Labour-Management Relations Series

Labour-Management Relations
in Public Enterprises
in Africa

International Labour Office **60**

Copyright © International Labour Organisation 1983

Publications of the International Labour Office enjoy copyright under Protocol 2 of the Universal Copyright Convention. Nevertheless, short excerpts from them may be reproduced without authorisation, on condition that the source is indicated. For rights of reproduction or translation, application should be made to the Publications Branch (Rights and Permissions), International Labour Office, CH-1211 Geneva 22, Switzerland. The International Labour Office welcomes such applications.

ISBN 92-2-103009-1
ISSN 0538-8325

First published 1983

The designations employed in ILO publications, which are in conformity with United Nations practice, and the presentation of material therein do not imply the expression of any opinion whatsoever on the part of the International Labour Office concerning the legal status of any country or territory or of its authorities, or concerning the delimitation of its frontiers.
The responsibility for opinions expressed in signed articles, studies and other contributions rests solely with their authors, and publication does not constitute an endorsement by the International Labour Office of the opinions expressed in them.

ILO publications can be obtained through major booksellers or ILO local offices in many countries, or direct from ILO Publications, International Labour Office, CH-1211 Geneva 22, Switzerland. A catalogue or list of new publications will be sent free of charge from the above address.

Printed by the International Labour Office, Geneva, Switzerland

TABLE OF CONTENTS

	Page
PREFACE	1
PART I: LABOUR-MANAGEMENT RELATIONS IN PUBLIC ENTERPRISES IN AFRICA	3
Definition of public enterprises	5
Reasons for the appearance and growth of public enterprises	7
Legal framework	10
Trade unions and employers' organisations	14
Trade unions	14
Employers' organisations	16
Collective bargaining	19
Dispute settlement	22
Personnel policies and practices	24
Workers' participation other than collective bargaining	26
Concluding remarks	28
PART II: NATIONAL MONOGRAPHS	31
Labour-management relations in public enterprises in Africa: the Nigerian case, by Professor T.M. Yesufu, Human Resources Research Unit, University of Lagos, Nigeria	33
Labour-management relations in Tunisian public enterprises, by N. Ladhari, Directorate of Social Security, Ministry of Social Affairs, Tunisia	57

PREFACE

In view of the increasing importance of public enterprises in the economy of many Third World countries, the ILO has recently engaged in a research project on labour-management relations in these enterprises in Asia, in Latin America and in Africa.

The studies undertaken in Asia and Latin America have already both led to publications.[1] The present issue of the Labour-Management Relations Series represents the outcome of the research conducted in Africa.

As far as the latter continent is concerned, national monographs have been prepared for a number of English-speaking as well as French-speaking countries by national external collaborators. On the basis of these monographs and of other material available, a brief comparative study has been prepared by the Labour Law and Labour Relations Branch of the ILO. This comparative study, written by Mr. Mesfin Gabre Michael, is reproduced in Part I of the present issue of the Labour-Management Relations Series. It had been the intention to reproduce in Part II all the national monographs available. In order to keep the number of pages of the present publication as well as its printing costs within certain limits, the Office had, however, to decide to publish only two monographs, one concerning an English-speaking country and one concerning a French-speaking country. The two monographs concerned are the one on Nigeria, prepared by Professor T.M. Yesufu, Human Resources Research Unit, University of Lagos, and the one on Tunisia, prepared by Mr. N. Ladhari, Directorate of Social Security of the Ministry of Social Affairs, Tunisia.

---

[1] For Asia, see: ILO-Friedrich-Ebert-Stiftung, Labour-Management Relations in Public Enterprises in Asia (Bangkok, 1978). For Latin America, see: OIT, Las relaciones laborales en las empresas estatales de América latina (publicado bajo la dirección de Arturo S. Bronstein) (Geneva, 1981).

PART I

LABOUR-MANAGEMENT RELATIONS IN
PUBLIC ENTERPRISES IN AFRICA

Comparative Study

Definition of public enterprises

In many African countries, today, public enterprises play a key role in national economic and social development. They have a strategic position in terms of the economic goods they produce as well as the various services they render, and they have gained increasing prominence because of the employment opportunities they create. The structure they have established to administer their labour force, and more specifically their labour-management relations machinery has also attracted the keen interest of African governments, employers and workers. Furthermore, in so far as it is generally recognised that the task of national development in African countries in the coming years cannot be left only to the civil service or the private sector, the future role of public enterprises would appear to be even greater. Correspondingly, the labour-management relations practices which develop in public enterprises will have a growing significance and will merit closer study and examination.

However, before an attempt is made to discuss the characteristics of labour-management relations in public enterprises, it is essential to try to define the term "public enterprise". What are public enterprises? How are they distinct from other undertakings? What are the boundaries between public enterprises and the civil service or the private sector?

Public enterprises exist in all African countries, with differences in size, scope of activities and forms of administration. Yet there appears to be no uniformly applicable definition to cover their distinct characteristics, especially as concerns labour-management relations. This is partly because each country establishes public enterprises for different purposes, and with different structures on the basis of its history, traditions, economic and social structure and political orientation. It is also partly due to the fact that within each country, the distinctions between public enterprises and other sectors with respect to their basic policies and internal control systems and, most of all, with respect to the day-to-day administrative practices - factors which directly affect labour-management relations - are often unclear. Consequently, the personality of public enterprises, the way they are viewed by the community and their objectives are sometimes indistinguishable from other enterprises.

Public enterprises are known under different names in different countries. For instance, many public enterprises are known as corporations in Nigeria, as "sociétés d'Etat" in Mali, as "sociétés nationales" in Senegal, as "parastatals" in Tanzania, or as "companies", "monopolies", "schemes", and in a number of other names in other countries. Nevertheless, none of these appellations fully covers all public enterprises so as to provide an adequate definition.

Aside from names and titles, the size and types of activities of undertakings may be considered as factors to identify public enterprises, and there might be a temptation to conclude that in many African countries large-scale undertakings and public utilities may account for most of them. And indeed in many cases, large-scale undertakings and public utilities are public enterprises. The Mining Company of Zaire (GECAMINES) and the Mining Corporation of Zambia, along with practically all the railway companies of all African countries, are only a few such examples. Nevertheless, public enterprises cover all types of undertakings ranging from vast agricultural plantations through large industrial corporations, down to small shops and services. In Nigeria, for example, one State Government even started a laundry service and several others entered the field of supermarkets. In Guinea and the Congo firms importing and exporting commercial commodities are public enterprises. Hence the mere size and the types of activities of an undertaking cannot provide sufficient elements for defining public enterprises.

From the legal point of view the term "public enterprise" does not appear to have been clearly defined so as to distinguish all public enterprises from other undertakings. Yet there are in practically all African countries, laws, administrative orders, guidelines and circulars governing certain public enterprises. For instance, in the Sudan, the Public Corporation Act of 1976 brings public undertakings under the control of the central Bureau for Public Corporations. Similarly, in Tanzania, the Public Corporations Act of 1969 empowers the President of the Republic to establish public corporations and define their structures, functions and management. Other countries, including Gabon, the Ivory Coast, Kenya and Sierra Leone, have set up public corporations and enacted special statutes for their administration in the form of joint stock companies, with governments as partial or major shareholders. However, while laws and guidelines directly refer to public enterprises, their coverage is not exhaustive. For example, the Public Corporation Act of 1976 in the Sudan does not cover the Gezira Irrigation Scheme, the biggest single public enterprise in the country. Hence, here again the term "public enterprise" is not satisfactorily defined by law. What, then, are the essential elements that give public enterprises the characteristics which distinguish them from other undertakings?

It might be possible to establish a rough-and-ready distinction between public enterprises and the private sector on the basis of ownership of capital. Stemming from that, another characteristic of public enterprises relates to the degree of public control and accountability. The State is responsible for the proper use of public resources and it cannot be a partial or a major owner of public enterprises and leave them without control. Confirming this view, the last six-year plan of the Sudan (1977/78-1982/83) states that "the viability of public enterprises systems essentially stems from the ability to combine the requirements of commercial autonomy and public accountability".[1] Still another characteristic might be the degree of managerial autonomy which is necessary if they are to take measures requiring speed in decision making, and which will allow them to take risks in order to cope with the demands of the market. In support of this point, the Nigerian Working Party on Statutory Corporations and State-owned Companies, 1966, reported that "the complexities of modern administration are such that the Government should, in its own interest, operate directly within limited fields, and should devise a machinery whereby its undertakings of a large-scale commercial and public utility character could operate with some measure of autonomy but under its general surveillance".[2]

---

[1] Six-Year Plan of the Republic of the Sudan (1977/78-1982/83), p. 52.

[2] Report of the Working Party on Statutory Corporations and State-owned Companies (Federal Ministry of Information, Lagos, 1966), p. 8.

In general, it can be said that public enterprises tend to behave like the civil service to the extent to which they are operated in the national interest or for the public welfare irrespective of profit and that they are inclined to adopt the behaviour of the private sector to the extent they endeavour to maximise their returns as do undertakings in that sector.

For the purpose of this study, the term "public enterprises" refers to all undertakings (agriculture, industry, commerce and transport) producing goods and supplying services which are totally or partially owned by the State. It excludes the civil service (central, regional and local administration or the State), and the private sector.

Reasons for the appearance and growth of public enterprises

To a large extent public enterprises were first established in Africa by the colonisers in order to promote the settlement of colonies and essentially to produce raw material to satisfy the economic demands of their markets. The British, for instance, started the Gezira Irrigation Scheme in the Sudan just after the First World War in order to satisfy their needs for cotton. In the late 1940s they also started the Tanganyika Groundnut Scheme as well as some 50 other similar schemes in their other African colonies.[1] The French started similar schemes in several of their colonies through concessions. The phosphate company in Tunisia and the railway systems in almost all the French colonies were started under such concessions. In Zaire, which was a Belgian colony, all mines became state property by order of King Leopold II.

Immediately after gaining political independence, mostly in the 1960s, African countries were confronted with the major and difficult task of acquiring economic independence as a prerequisite for the creation of self-reliant States. However, they did not have adequate industrial infrastructure and know-how to meet development requirements. Moreover, local prospective entrepreneurs who would be expected to act as agents of rapid growth and development were initially too weak to embark on big-scale operations that could have significant impact on a national scale. Hence, the States had to commit themselves to nation building by establishing development plans and targets which entailed, inter alia, the creation of state-owned or state-controlled economic ventures - public enterprises.

Unlike the rationale for development in socialist countries (Eastern Europe), where it is believed that the establishment and growth of state ownership of capital is a prelude to socialism, the philosophical basis for nationalisation and the development of public enterprises in African countries cannot be entirely attributed to the socialist ideology, nor has it necessarily been capitalist-inspired. It was in a large measure a spontaneous and pragmatic phenomenon, due to the wish to find an expedient way of achieving economic and social development within a short time and with limited

---

[1] Ioan Davies: <u>African Trade Unions</u> (Harmondsworth, Middlesex, England, 1966), p. 18.

resources. However, one should not forget that many economic development measures and strategies adopted by these States in the process of nation building, including the development of public enterprises, were promoted in the context of specific political and philosophical principles. Hence, the creation of public enterprises found its philosophical basis in "Nkrumahism" in Ghana, in "Harambee" in Kenya, in "Ujamaa" in Tanzania, in "Islamic Socialism" in Libya, in "participation responsable" in Senegal, in "L'Authenticité" in Zaire, in "Humanism" in Zambia and in many other political ideologies in other African countries.

In general terms, the setting up of public enterprises is designed to ensure that the aims of national economic plans are adequately met. More specifically the main reasons for the creation of public enterprises are the following:

(1) to provide the necessary infrastructural conditions for the private sector to operate properly and to render services and utilities which otherwise could not be created by the private sector.

Thus, in Nigeria, which has a mixed economy with an inclination towards private capitalism, the emphasis in the development of public enterprises is on assistance to the private sector and the creation of certain conditions in which it can operate efficiently. Hence, public enterprises, and the public sector in general, are expected among others to provide the necessary infrastructural facilities to enable private enterprises to operate and to supplement private enterprise investment activity where this is not forthcoming adequately or promptly.[1] In Tunisia, the Government had, upon independence, to create public enterprises in all sectors of the economy, in order to meet the manpower and economic needs of the society. Some of these public enterprises were the National Company for Navigation, the National Society for Real Estate, the National Press Agency as well as National Commercial Offices.

(2) To acquire sufficient capital to meet development targets and to ensure that capital so acquired is reinvested to generate employment and fulfil other national plans and strategies.

That is why, for example, the late President of the Republic of Botswana, in a speech, stated that "... if development and economic growth are to benefit the majority of our people, and if we are to maintain the social stability which is essential for economic growth to continue, we must see that the resources generated by mining development (a major public enterprise) are mainly reinvested and not consumed".[2] In Cameroon, the National Society for Investment adopted certain fiscal policies and other measures, in order to encourage savings and enhance investment by nationals in agriculture, commerce and industry.[3]

---

[1] O. Aboyade: Nigerian Public Enterprises as an Organisational Dilemma, Public Enterprises in Nigeria, Proceedings of the 1973 Annual Conference of the Nigerian Economic Society (Lagos, 1974), p. 33.

[2] Sir Seretse Khama, President of the Republic of Botswana, Address to the Botswana Trade Union Education Centre's Cornerstone Ceremony, 10 July 1971.

[3] G.L. Djeudjang: "Le role des societés dans le developpement economique de La République Unie du Cameroun", Revue Juridique et Politique - Indépendance et Coopération (Paris), No. 1, Jan.-Mar. 1978, p. 228.

(3) To indigenise the economy and to fill the vacuum created upon the departure of the colonisers.

For example, Zambia, which was known as Northern Rhodesia prior to independence, had a federal structure of colonial rule with Southern Rhodesia, now Zimbabwe. During the colonial period most of the strategic common services, including the Central African Airways and the Kariba Power Station, were concentrated in the then Southern Rhodesia. Even the secondary industries that were developed during colonial rule had their base in Southern Rhodesia, while Northern Rhodesia (Zambia) had only subsidiaries. After independence in 1964, and especially after the Unilateral Declaration of Independence of Southern Rhodesia in 1965, followed by the United Kingdom economic blockade on the latter, Zambia was left with hardly any services and utilities or infrastructure. In January 1965, it had to launch an emergency development programme with the primary objective of filling the vacuum left by the break-up of the Federation.[1]

(4) To avoid scarcity of commodities which are essential to the consumption pattern of the market and to control prices.

Examples of this are the relatively small government-owned trade corporations in many countries, including Ghana, Guinea, Liberia, Mali, Nigeria, Tanzania and Uganda, which import and distribute scarce food items, such as rice, flour and sugar, and attempt to control the rate of inflation.

Whatever form the historical development of public enterprises in African countries may take, their numbers have been constantly on the increase since independence. They have expanded in size and in the types of economic activities they cover. Accordingly, their role in the social and economic development of the respective States has become more vital. Precise over-all figures on the exact importance of public enterprises in different African countries are not readily available, but it is not difficult to mention examples which provide a general idea of the magnitude and importance of public enterprises. For example, a single public enterprise (the Gezira Irrigation Scheme) accounts for more than 60 per cent of the cotton produced in the Sudan. The Sudanese cotton sector is a big exporter, and employs over half a million workers including those employed on a seasonal basis. This is close to 30 per cent of the labour force in the modern sector. In Senegal the labour force employed in the public sector was estimated to be only 26,000 in 1978 but the salaries earned by this labour force represented about 25 per cent of the total wage bill in the country.[2]

In the area of labour-management relations, it is of relevance to note that in many African countries only a small portion of the economically active population are wage earners. The large

---

[1] The Federation of Northern and Southern Rhodesia was declared in 1953. Northern Rhodesia gained independence in 1964 and became Zambia. In 1965, Southern Rhodesia unilaterally declared its independence (UDI) and remained so until 1979 when it became Zimbabwe.

[2] Institut d'études politiques de Bordeaux-Centre d'étude d'Afrique Noire, Les entreprises publiques en Afrique Noire (ed. A. Pédones, Paris, 1980), Tome I, p. 15.

majority live in the rural areas mostly on subsistence agriculture. Among the wage earners, the organisable labour force is reduced by legal and other limitations, which in some instances prohibit unions in the civil service, domestic service and certain essential services or set out stringent requirements for the establishment of workers' organisations. For instance, in several countries, including Kenya, Somalia and the Sudan, a minimum of 50 workers would be legally required in an undertaking before they can organise a union. Given the fact that many undertakings in Africa are relatively small, employing in many cases less than 50 workers, this requirement may no doubt prevent the workers from organising. These conditions would tend to lead to the conclusion that public enterprises in many African countries may actually be the biggest employers of organised labour, thereby confirming their strategic position in the area of labour-management relations. The parts which follow will attempt to briefly examine the labour-management relations problems and practices in African countries.

Legal framework

With a few exceptions most African countries were either British or French colonies or protectorates. As such they have inherited British and French labour laws and to a great extent followed labour relations models designed for them by these powers. As a consequence, labour laws in countries formerly under the jurisdiction of either of these powers were initially similar and labour-management relations practices, whether in the private sector or in public enterprises, relied heavily on free collective bargaining.

After independence these countries faced the major task of economic and social development, and in their efforts to meet these challenges introduced legal reforms which were thought to reflect their national characteristics and to be consistent with the goals their respective governments had outlined. Some countries, like Ghana and Tanzania, were quick to introduce radical changes, while others, like the Ivory Coast, Kenya, Senegal, Sierra Leone and Togo, introduced reforms relatively gradually. Nevertheless, even with drastic changes and reforms, the remnants of British or French labour legislation can still be observed in most, if not all, of the African countries.

Many African countries have a general legal framework which provides workers with the right to organise and to bargain collectively. Approximately 15 countries, including Cameroon, Gabon, the Ivory Coast, Senegal, Togo, Tunisia and Zaire, have fully fledged labour codes containing provisions on the right to organise and to bargain collectively. A growing number of countries, such as Ghana, Mauritius, Sierra Leone and Zambia, have adopted specific industrial relations Acts which also recognise the right of employers and workers to organise themselves and to negotiate terms and conditions of employment. Other countries, like Ethiopia, the Sudan and Tanzania, have enacted trade union Acts or trade dispute Acts, employees' Acts or similar legislation, which also guarantee the right to organise and bargain collectively.

However, there are no African countries which have separate labour laws covering all public enterprises as envisaged in this study. The legislation which applies to other sectors also governs labour-management relations in public enterprises. In this respect, public enterprises may be grouped in three categories: those which are within government departments and which are normally covered by the legislation applying to the civil service; those which are registered companies in which the State has shares and which are generally governed by the same legislation as private companies; and those which are statutory corporations and which come usually either under special legislation or partly under civil service legislation and partly under private company law.

In Egypt, for instance, Act No. 32 of 1966 respecting public corporations and companies of the public sector as amended in 1977 gives power to every ministry to establish and administer public corporations and companies. In the Sudan, the Employees' Discipline Act of 1976 and the Public Service Pension Act of 1977 apply to certain public enterprises (public corporations) and the civil service. Similarly in Zaire, the Labour Code gives a definition of "employer" and "employees" which are equally applicable to the civil service and public enterprises.

Practically all African countries have public corporations governed by special statutes as well as others which function as registered companies in which the States have shares.

However, the fact that public companies are governed by a given legislation is not in itself a precise indication of the real extent of government involvement in labour-management relations practices. In most African countries labour-management relations in public enterprises governed by private company law may, in comparison with the private sector, be generally characterised by greater government intervention and restriction of voluntarism with regard to the activities of organised labour and procedures for settlement of labour disputes. In contrast, practices in public enterprises which are governed by civil service legislation may be more liberal than those in the civil service properly speaking. In many cases, civil servants may not be allowed to organise themselves into unions or there may be severe restrictions on unionisation, while employees of public enterprises may be allowed to form their own unions. Industrial action such as strikes, is generally prohibited both in the civil service and in public enterprises assimilated to the civil service; if, however, it occurs, it is likely to be more tolerated in public enterprises than in the civil service proper.

It thus appears that there are always differences between public enterprises and the other sectors of the economy with respect to labour-management relations practices. It would be of interest to examine the reasons and the legal basis of these distinctions.

At the outset, it ought to be recognised that the extent to which labour-management relations practices in public enterprises differ from those in other sectors depends first of all on the political and social stability of a country, including the form of government that may be in power. As has been common experience in many countries, a centralised government will tend to take stringent measures to maintain control of undertakings which render vital economic and social services. Labour-management relations in these undertakings, many of which may be public enterprises, will be directly affected by such measures. In this connection it is also worth noting that about 40 per cent of African countries have experienced military rule and about 50 per cent of these countries, or about 20 per cent of all the African countries, are still under military rule. Declarations of states of emergency, which have at times lasted for lengthy periods, have also been frequent in these countries. These conditions have, as a rule, directly affected the system of labour relations in general and labour-management relations in public enterprises in particular. In countries which are still under military rule the trade union laws have been tightened and the machinery for dealing with industrial disputes has been reinforced. This was, for example, the case in Nigeria, whose traditional voluntary industrial relations policy was modified during the Civil War (1967-70) and during the following period of national emergency which was lifted only in 1978. Examples of similar experiences could be cited from Benin, Ghana, Madagascar, the Seychelles, Somalia, the Sudan and Uganda.

Another factor affecting labour relations may be the role public enterprises play in national economy and how essential are the products and services they supply. If, as is often the case, public enterprises are engaged in the production of commodities which are crucial to the economy in terms of generating employment or producing major export items, the importance attached to them by the government and other authorities is likely to be high; the disruption of harmonious labour relations becomes a public issue and every effort is made to restore order by voluntary and if necessary compulsory conciliatory measures. For instance, in practically all African countries transport services, as essential services, are given greater attention than, say, textile factories, in their labour-management relations practices.

The distinctions or peculiarities in the practice of labour-management relations in public enterprises are mostly introduced on the basis of legal or administrative provisions. In some countries the labour laws have specific provisions to exclude certain public enterprises from their coverage. In Nigeria, for instance, the Trade Unions Decree of 1973 specifically bars the Nigerian Printing and Minting Company Limited and the Nigerian External Telecommunications Limited from organising or belonging to trade unions.

In some countries labour laws have provisions which allow an executive body to limit or expand the application of the law at its discretion by including certain undertakings or institutions in the scope of the laws or by exempting them therefrom. This may provide a legal basis for creating distinctions in the practice of labour-management relations. In Tanzania, for instance, the extent and scope of application of some parts of the Security of Employment Act, 1964, are to be determined by the Minister of Labour. The Minister may, by notice published in the Gazette, apply Part IV of this Act, which deals with termination of employment, to Tanzania generally or may restrict its application to any part of Tanzania, or any category or description (however defined) of business or employers.[1] The Zambia Industrial Relations Act of

---

[1] ILO: Legislative Series, 1964 - Tan. 2, Article 2.

1971 states that "The provisions of this Act shall apply to any public or local <u>authority</u> only to such an extent and such manner and from such date or dates as the President may, by statutory instrument, prescribe for that purpose."[1] Depending on the meaning of the term "authority", public enterprises may easily be excluded from the scope of the Industrial Relations Act. In Senegal the Labour Code states that "the provisions of this Chapter (that means the chapter on settlement of collective disputes) ... shall not apply to wage earners in public services, undertakings and establishments unless there are no provisions of law or regulations to the contrary".[2]

Such provisions are especially common in the area of essential services. It should be noted in this connection that, while a good number of public enterprises are essential services, not all essential services are public enterprises or vice versa. The demarcation between the two is often not clear and there appears to be a high degree of overlapping. The legal provisions applicable to essential services take into account the concept of "essentiality" and impose restrictive measures on the practice of labour-management relations; these measures usually prohibit industrial action such as strikes and lockouts. Many African countries have schedules of essential services included in their legislations. Some of these countries have also given power to an executive body to set out these schedules without any prior approval of a legislative body. Thus, for example, in Kenya, the Minister of Labour may, by a notice in the national gazette, declare "any particular undertaking, activity or business as being included in an essential service".[3] Similar provisions are included in the Regulation of Wages and Industrial Relations Act, 1971, of Sierra Leone and in the Trade Unions and Trade Disputes Ordinance of Zambia, 1965. In Cameroon, where there is no schedule of essential services, the administrative authorities are authorised to requisition, individually or collectively, workers involved in any strike undertaken in a vital sector of economic, social or cultural activity.[4] There are similar provisions in Senegal and Tunisia. Such provisions make it easy for an executive body to declare public enterprises which do not actually meet the characteristics of "essentiality" to be included in the schedule of essential services and thereby deprive them of the right to take industrial action.

Distinctive patterns in labour-management relations practices in public enterprises may be founded on still other approaches. In order to ensure efficiency and adequate production, an executive body may issue administrative orders and directives to public enterprises. Although these directives do not necessarily contradict the provisions of the national laws they may, nevertheless, introduce specific requirements and procedures into the day-to-day operations of the undertakings and may even result in special patterns of labour-management relations there. Such administrative directives may deal with a wide range of subjects, including wages, questions related to labour disputes, detailed procedures for

---

[1] ILO: <u>Legislative Series</u>, 1971 - Zam. 2, Part I, section 2, subsection (2).

[2] ibid., 1962 - Sen. 2, Chapter II, Article 231.

[3] ibid., 1965 - Ken. 1, Part V, Article 34(1).

[4] ibid., 1974 - Cam. 1, Article 165(3).

collective bargaining, holidays and absenteeism. In Ethiopia, for example, an internal directive passed by the Government has tentatively fixed a minimum wage for workers in public enterprises and has set out detailed procedures for negotiation of collective agreements. In Tanzania, Presidential Circular No. 1, 1970, gives directives on the establishment of workers' councils, executive boards and boards of directors in parastatal organisations.

In a number of other countries some ad hoc bodies with power to decide on specific aspects of labour-management relations have been set up. The decisions of these bodies may establish further basis for government action and thereby create distinct characteristics in the labour-management relations of public enterprises. In Nigeria, for instance, a Commission known as the Udoji Commission, which was appointed in 1972 and which worked until the end of 1974, determined wages, retirement benefits and leave periods for the public sector. The decisions of this Commission are said to have created disparities between public enterprises and the private sector which were to have a major impact on the national system of labour-management relations in the following years.

Trade unions and employers' organisations

Trade unions

Historically, trade unions of public enterprises have been the spearhead of trade union movements in Africa. In many English-speaking countries, including Ethiopia, Kenya, Nigeria, Sierra Leone, the Sudan, Tanzania and Zambia, the first trade unions ever to be organised came from railway companies.[1] In other countries like Gambia and Ghana the first trade unions were in the shipyards and in the mines respectively - both of which are usually public enterprises. In many French-speaking African countries, including Congo, Niger and Senegal, trade unionism in the public sector started around 1937 whereas workers in the private sector had to wait until 1946 before their organisation could take shape and develop.[2] In most African countries it was actually public enterprises which started the process of industrialisation and the fact that trade unions were also first organised in them might further confirm the contention that labour relations can only be viewed as a component of a greater system of industrialisation.

Most African countries allow employees of most public enterprises to form trade unions or to become members of existing unions. In a few countries employees of certain public enterprises are, along with the civil service and the armed forces, prohibited from organising in trade unions for the purposes of collective bargaining and other industrial action. In Liberia, for example, until recently the labour laws prohibited government employees from organising in unions. In practice the meaning of "government employees" was extended to include employees of public enterprises who would otherwise have been free to form unions: a total of about 21 public corporations (public enterprises) employing about

---

[1] David C. Ojeli: Industrial Relations in English-speaking West Africa, International Institute for Labour Studies (Geneva, 1976), p. 21.

[2] Gilbert Pongault: "Trade Unionism and the Public Services in Africa", Labor (Bruxelles) 2, 1967, p. 64.

10,000 workers were affected and consequently barred from forming or belonging to trade unions.[1]

Aside from such exceptions, employees in public enterprises of African countries have the right to form or join trade unions on the same terms and conditions as employees in the private sector. The legal requirements for the formation of trade unions in the private sector apply to public enterprises. These requirements, which are basically similar in many countries, are designed principally to ensure that trade unions are democratically formed and that they are the legitimate representatives of their members.

For instance, in Nigeria, Somalia and in the Sudan not less than 50 workers are required to subscribe to a trade union application for registration. In Zambia, an application for registration may be made to the Commissioner of Labour by not less than seven members of the trade union. The application must be signed by its members and a copy submitted to the Zambia Congress of Trade Unions. In most French-speaking African countries, including Gabon, Mali and Senegal, a minimum of 25 members are required before a trade union is legally recognised. In the majority of cases, including Egypt, Ethiopia, Ghana, Liberia, Nigeria, Somalia and Zambia, only one union may be formed in an undertaking.

In the Sudan the Employees and Trade Union Act, 1977, classifies trade unions into three categories - workers' unions, officials' unions and professionals' unions and provides definitions for the terms "worker", "official" and "professional". In each category distinctions are made between the public and the private sectors, such that there are separate workers', officials' and professionals' unions in the public as well as the private sectors. However, as all public enterprises are not included in the public sector, their employees are organised under the three categories in both the public and the private sectors. Only one union of each category is allowed in one industry. In Tanzania the "JUWATA" Act, 1979, established JUWATA (Tanzania workers' organisation) as a unitary organisation with branches in every industry. To facilitate its administration JUWATA has created seven industrial sections, and employees of public enterprises are organised as branches under the different sections.

An examination of the national structures of trade unions in African countries reveals that in many cases there are no separate unions for public enterprises. Trade unions are predominantly organised as general or industry unions, drawing their membership from both public enterprises and the private sector, or even, in exceptional cases, from government agencies. For instance, the Nigerian Union of Journalists includes in its membership journalists from state and federal newspapers as well as their colleagues in privately owned enterprises. Similarly, in Zambia, the hotel and restaurant services' national union has members from both the private sector and public enterprises. Similar examples can be found in other countries. In some cases, however, particular classes of employees in public enterprises may form their own unions to the exclusion of members from other sectors. This is mostly due to the nature of their work, but is not a matter of policy derived

---

[1] H. Astrand: _Employers' Analysis of the Labour Laws_, paper submitted to the Second National Tripartite Conference - Government, Management, Labour (Monrovia, Dec. 1978), p. 2.

from their status as public employees. Port and mine workers' unions in Ghana, Nigeria, Sierra Leone and the Mine Workers' Union in Zambia, as well as the railway workers' unions in practically all of the African countries, are examples of unions having membership only from public enterprises.

Some examples from public enterprises in some countries may give an idea of the numbers and proportion of organised workers in public enterprises. On the whole, because of the vital political and economic importance of public enterprises their workers tend to be effectively organised into unions. In many countries the level of trade union organisation is much higher in public enterprises than in the private sector and trade unions in public enterprises account for the bulk of the membership of national trade union centres. In the area of transport, especially railways, it appears that there is a very high level of trade union organisation. Railway workers' unions have frequently over 90 per cent of the total workers employed in railway corporations in their membership. This is the case in Ethiopia, Ghana, Kenya, Nigeria, the Sudan and Zambia.

In most African countries trade unions in public enterprises can affiliate to national trade union centres, either directly or through a national industrial union. In some countries, such as Ghana and Zambia, trade unions automatically become members of the national trade union centres - the Ghana Congress of Trade Unions and the Zambia Congress of Trade Unions - immediately after their formation. In many countries, trade unions in public enterprises constitute a significant proportion of the membership of national trade union centres and trade union leaders from public enterprises often assume very high positions in the leadership of organised labour nationally.

Employers' organisations

In most African countries, employers' organisations at the national level have a much more recent origin than trade unions. The few national employers' organisations which had a relatively early start were the Association of Egyptian Industries which was established as early as 1922, the Union intersyndicale d'entreprises et d'industries de l'Ouest Africain (UNISYNDI) of Senegal in 1944, the Union Tunisienne du l'industrie, du commerce et de l'artisanat (UTICA) in 1946, the Nigerian Employers' Consultative Association founded in 1957 and the Union interprofessionelle du Gabon as well as the Ghana Employers' Association and the Federation of Kenya Employers, all of which started in 1959. Many other African national employers' organisations came into existence in the 1960s.

The position of the management of public enterprises in national employers' organisations has not been the same in all these countries. In some countries, public enterprises actually formed the embryo of employers' organisations and continue to constitute the majority of their membership. In others, managements of public enterprises played little, if any, part in founding organisations of employers, and were, and still in some cases are, excluded from full membership in national employers' organisations.

In Liberia, for instance, the three employers' organisations, the Rubber Planters' Association, the Chamber of Commerce, and the Miners' Association, are open to all persons or companies engaged in their respective areas of competence, i.e., rubber planting and/or processing, commerce and mining. Considering the fact that the rubber industry and mining are two of the major public enterprises in the country, one can safely deduce that employers' organisations in Liberia are in effect largely dominated by public enterprises. Similarly, in Sierra Leone the Employers' Federation of Sierra Leone was created by the amalgamation of the Sierra Leone African Chamber of Commerce and the Sierra Leone Mining Association. The contribution of the mining industry, which is a major public enterprise in the country, is self-evident.

In the majority of African countries, including Botswana, Burundi, Egypt, Kenya, Malawi, Nigeria, Tunisia, Uganda, Zaire and Zambia, public enterprises are full members of the respective national employers' organisations. They contribute to the programmes and activities of these organisations as do employers from the private sector. However, in a few African countries, even though they have the right to join national employers' organisations, public enterprises have been hesitant to do so. In Nigeria, for instance, public enterprises are free to belong to the Nigerian Employers' Consultative Association; yet some, particularly those responsible for public utilities, hardly see any reason to do so. When they join they often do so as associates rather than full members.

In a few countries, public enterprises do not have full membership in national employers' organisations. Such countries include Cameroon, Ghana, Lesotho, Mauritius and the Sudan. In these countries the respective national employers' organisations only allow public enterprises the status of associate membership, usually without the right of electing or being elected for leadership. Certain national employers' organisations have limited their membership to the private sector. The Union patronale et interprofessionelle du Congo (UNICONGO), the Groupement des Entreprises privées de Madagascar are two examples of such employers' organisations.[1]

In a few countries, e.g., Algeria, Ethiopia and Somalia, employers' organisations hardly exist. In Ethiopia the Federation of Ethiopian Employers was ordered to be closed by a ministerial letter in January 1978 after 14 years of active existence. Since then, the Ethiopian Chamber of Commerce, which is mostly composed of managers of public enterprises, has been representing employers at the International Labour Conference. In Somalia, an organisation of employers has not yet been established. The Chamber of Commerce of Somalia registers all industries in its membership but is never known to have had a role in the area of labour relations.

The role of public enterprises in the programmes and activities of employers' organisations and consequently in labour-management relations may be viewed from various angles. Obviously public enterprises will have a greater role to play in those employers' organisations where they have full membership and even more so in those where they make up the majority of the membership. Correspondingly, their impact will be much weaker where they are only associate members.

---

[1] BIT: "Rôle des organisations d'employeurs dans les pays d'Afrique francophone", Série relations professionnelles, No. 46 (Geneva, 1974), pp. 53 and 86.

The labour relations programmes and activities of employers' organisations may be carried out in three different areas:
(1) employers' organisations usually have educational and information programmes for their membership and may at times give general guidelines to their members on certain questions of labour relations;
(2) employers' organisations may have direct contacts with trade unions at various levels, including the national level, with a view to the conclusion of collective agreement or the settlement of labour disputes; (3) employers' organisations usually establish direct contacts with governments as well and try to embody what they consider to be essential elements of labour relations in the laws and procedures of government.

In almost all African countries, employers' organisations are carrying out educational and information programmes in the industrial relations field for the benefit of their members, including public enterprises.

In their relations with trade unions, employers' organisations have adopted different practices ranging from informal meetings and consultations to formal agreements. In most African countries employers' organisations assist their members from the private and the public sectors in the negotiation of agreements and the settlement of disputes.

In Nigeria, for instance, the Nigerian Employers' Consultative Association provides non-binding advisory services to its members. In Kenya and most of the French-speaking African countries, the employers' organisations assist members in their proceedings at the Industrial Court. In some countries, including Kenya, Sierra Leone, Tunisia and Zaire, the employers' organisations take part in collective bargaining and have concluded agreements, covering both the private and the public sector, with the trade union at the national level.

As far as the relations with governments are concerned, representatives of private and public enterprises have, through employers' organisations, been recognised as the representatives of employers and given various opportunities to present their position together with workers' representatives. They are made members of advisory boards, committees and many other permanent and ad hoc bodies to help improve the systems and practices of labour relations. Some are even represented in judiciary boards for labour disputes. When public enterprises are full members, many of the representatives of employers' organisations are actually from public enterprises. In addition, many employers' organisations also monitor, on a continuous basis, all initiatives of government in the industrial relations field and take action, whenever necessary, to safeguard the interests of their members.

Collective bargaining[1]

While collective bargaining was largely introduced into African countries by the colonising powers, mainly the British and the French, it quickly acquired its own characteristics and dynamics. Initially, it was to a great extent based on the premise that the parties were free to negotiate wages and working conditions while national labour laws established minimum standards. However, the difficulties of economic development prompted some important changes and the tradition of free collective bargaining began to give way in some countries to more controlled systems where much is determined through national legislations or other government measures. In a way this is not surprising, because in African countries, as in most other developing countries, many social and economic activities, including collective bargaining, are always seen in the light of the prevailing urge for rapid development and progress. The Tanzanian view of collective bargaining, for instance, is geared to encompass the political aspirations of building a socialist society, with the consequence that statutory provisions determine the parameters for collective bargaining in all public enterprises. In another country, Kenya, collective bargaining is also influenced to some extent by the Government, especially with regard to certain issues such as wages, but the influence is exerted with the objective of achieving a compromise in the practice of labour relations in which state power is mostly used to channel market forces towards the achievement of certain economic objectives.

In nearly all cases, the obvious organs for collective bargaining in public enterprises are trade unions. However, in some countries like Nigeria, the Sudan and Zambia, the law permits, in the absence of trade unions, the setting up of consultative committees through which workers and management can bargain on matters related to terms and conditions of services. In the Sudan, the Industrial Relations Act of 1976 allows employees in public enterprises without unions to carry out collective bargaining through representative committees. In public enterprises where there are trade unions, the same law prohibits the involvement in collective bargaining of any other body except the trade unions. In Zambia, collective bargaining in public enterprises without trade unions is conducted also by committees made up of representatives of employees and employers. In most French-speaking African countries, the labour codes stipulate that collective bargaining aimed at what is known as "ordinary" collective agreement can take place between a group of workers (occupational association or other de facto groups such as a strike committee) on the one hand and an employers' organisation or a single employer on the other. In some countries, such as the Central African Republic, enterprise agreements may also be concluded by the staff delegates in public enterprises.

In many African countries, collective bargaining took place until recently mainly at the plant level, the most common practice being bargaining between the management of a public enterprise and the corresponding plant union. However, with the amalgamation of

---

[1] The term "collective bargaining" is used in a broad context, not only with reference to negotiations of agreements on wages and working conditions but also as a process for accommodation of different interests.

plant unions into industrial unions, collective bargaining is
slowly shifting in some countries to the industry level. This is,
for instance, the case in Ghana, Mauritania, Senegal, Tunisia and
Zaire. In Nigeria, the Labour Congress issued in 1980 a document
containing both a discussion of national issues and a list of
specific demands concerning working conditions which should guide
negotiations at lower levels.

Nevertheless, the role of the plant or local union in the
process of collective bargaining is still crucial in many African
countries. Representatives from local unions are often involved
in the negotiations at the industry level and collective agreements
entered into by industrial unions are often subject to approval by
the membership at the local level.

In some countries, including Kenya, Sierra Leone and Zambia,
collective bargaining takes place at all three levels, i.e., wages
are negotiated at the national level with active government
involvement, other general matters are negotiated at the industrial
level and more detailed terms and conditions of employment peculiar
to each public enterprise are negotiated at the undertaking or
plant level.

In many French-speaking African countries, industry-wide
bargaining is prevalent. However, in many cases the industry may
consist of only one public enterprise. In addition, the industry-
wide agreements are often supplemented by single public enterprise
agreements. This is, for instance, the case in the Ivory Coast,
Mauritania, Niger, Tunisia and Zaire.

The procedures for collective bargaining vary from one country
to another. In the majority of cases, collective bargaining is
initiated by trade unions. In some countries, like Kenya and
Sierra Leone, the procedures for collective bargaining are to a
large extent left to be determined by the parties. In some other
countries, including Ethiopia, Ghana and Zambia, there are legal
provisions establishing a duty to bargain for employers and trade
unions under a threat of penalties. In Ethiopia, where negotiations take place at the undertaking level, the laws list the
subjects for collective bargaining in a general way. In Zambia
the law requires that a recognition agreement be signed by the
two parties and provides for the methods and procedures under which
the agreement may be altered, replaced or terminated.[1]

Under the labour codes of many of the French-speaking African
countries, collective bargaining in public enterprises can take
place directly between the parties without following any prescribed
forms, where such bargaining is aimed at the conclusion of an
"ordinary" collective agreement. However, upon the request of one
of the parties or on the initiative of the government authorities,
the latter may convene the parties to negotiate under the procedure
for negotiating "collective agreements subject to extension".
This entails the setting up by governmental or ministerial decree
of joint committees composed of equal numbers of representatives
of the management and the trade union.

---

[1] ILO: Legislative Series, 1971 - Zam. 2, Article 112.

The concept of disclosure of information to trade unions for collective bargaining purposes is not very widely known. However, in some cases, such as Ethiopia, Tanzania and Zambia, the right to obtain relevant information is directly or indirectly provided for by law for all undertakings, including public enterprises. In Ethiopia, trade unions in public enterprises are empowered by law to discuss issues concerning productivity and fulfilment of enterprise targets, and therefore need to have access to all information. In Tanzania, the Permanent Labour Tribunal Act imposes penal sanctions on the management of a public enterprise which unreasonably withholds from the local union information directly relevant to the issues being negotiated. In Zambia, the works councils have a legal right to request information on the functioning of a public enterprise.

As concerns the status and application of collective agreements, in practically all African countries collective agreements, once concluded and registered with the appropriate government organ, have come to be considered as legally binding documents and part of the employment contract. It should, however, be noted that the registration process, where it exists, plays an important role in that it allows a check on the agreement for violation of guidelines and policies, especially with regard to wages. In essence, the government, through the process of verification and registration, endorses the agreement and makes it enforceable. In Kenya, for instance, an employer who implements any provision of a collective agreement or the relevant part of any existing collective agreement which has not been registered by the Industrial Court is guilty of an offence and is liable to fine. In the Sudan, there is no legal provision stipulating that collective agreements are binding. However, a decision recently given by the Attorney-General makes all registered collective agreements legally binding.

The duration of collective agreements in English-speaking African countries normally ranges from two to three years and hardly exceeds four years. In some countries such as Ethiopia and Zambia, the duration has been determined by law. In French-speaking African countries collective agreements of unspecified duration are the current practice.

Some reference has already been made to the scope of negotiable issues. The central question that arises in this connection is the degree of autonomy that public enterprises should have in the process of collective bargaining. Obviously, one of the main reasons for establishing public enterprises outside the civil service is to give them some degree of autonomy in planning their activities, allowing them flexibility in adjusting to market needs and enabling them to develop a system of administration comparable in efficiency to the private sector. In many African countries, this autonomy is limited by government policies and guidelines. Many African governments have issued national guidelines on employment, wages and incomes policies. For example, a Presidential Directive issued in Kenya at the beginning of 1979 required all public enterprises to increase their wage earning labour force by 10 per cent,[1] thereby determining the level of employment irrespective of what the labour market conditions may be.

---

[1] Annual Report of the Federation of Kenya Employers, 1979, p. 11.

In many African countries wage determination is an area where collective bargaining in public enterprises may have relatively little influence. The determination of wages often entails government intervention, at times to the point of excluding it as a subject for collective bargaining and making it the sole responsibility of the government. Governments in many African countries, in the face of high levels of unemployment and high rates of inflation, find it necessary to bring the determination of wages under some kind of control and supervision. The supervision and control have taken different forms. In certain countries, e.g., Botswana, Gambia, Kenya, Morocco, Senegal, Zaire and Zambia, the legislation provides that collective agreements can be valid only when the relevant government body registers them after verifying that government policies and guidelines, with respect to wages and other matters, have been complied with. Another form of government intervention is to impose a compulsory wage freeze or to limit wage increases to a certain percentage (higher ceilings being generally fixed for wage increases to lower paid workers). For instance, in Nigeria, the Federal Government has come out with a policy on wages and salaries for 1980-82. According to this policy, negotiations for wages and salary increases in all undertakings including public enterprises cannot exceed 15 per cent for lower income groups and 10 per cent for high income groups.[1] Similarly, in Kenya, wage guidelines issued in February 1979 provided, among other things, that over-all wage increases should average no more than 50 per cent of the rise in the cost of living provided that higher increases should be allowed for lower paid workers.[2]

This is not to say, however, that collective bargaining is completely left out of the wage determination process. In some French-speaking African countries, a distinction is made between the minimum wages fixed by governments and the over-all wage structure (real wages) which is supposed to be determined by collective bargaining. In Morocco and Zaire, for instance, the latter usually takes place at the enterprise level. In other countries, wage negotiations are carried out at the industry-wide level as in Tunisia, or within joint national committees on collective bargaining and wages, as in Cameroon.[3]

Nevertheless, the degree of autonomy which public enterprises, the largest employers of organised labour, should have in the process of collective bargaining while at the same time retaining responsibility to government development targets remains a central issue in every African country.

Dispute settlement

Most African legislations do not make distinctions between disputes of interests and disputes of rights. However, a considerable number of African countries recognise the advantage of

---

[1] West Africa (London), Apr. 1980, p. 758.

[2] Annual Report of the Federation of Kenya Employers, 1979, p. 9.

[3] See BIT: "Les salaires dans les pays d'Afrique francophone", Série Relations professionnelles, No. 55 (Geneva, 1978), pp. 15, 62, 69.

establishing suitable grievance procedures as an essential element of sound labour-management relations. Accordingly, legislations in a number of countries, including Ethiopia, Ghana and Zambia, have in one way or another prescribed the establishment of grievance procedures. In others - Cameroon, Guinea, the Ivory Coast, Senegal, Togo and in nearly all other French-speaking African countries - staff representatives have been instituted for similar purposes. Under this system workers' representatives elected by personnel of public enterprises are assigned the main function of presenting workers' grievances to management. In Liberia, Part IV of Title 194 of the 1956 Code provided for the establishment of grievance committees in enterprises above 20 employees.

In other countries grievance procedures are spelt out in collective agreements. Under the Kenya Industrial Relations Charter, agreed upon by the Government of Kenya, the Federation of Kenya Employers and the Central Organisation of Trade Unions, provision is made for strict observance of the grievance procedure set out in the Recognition Agreement between the parties. In Sierra Leone, the Industrial Relations Charter has established a framework for peaceful resolution of grievances through trade group councils.

Grievance procedures involving successive steps at different levels are most common in large-scale public enterprises. In general, the procedures for dispute settlement and the nature of disputes in public enterprises vary from one enterprise to another depending on the size of the enterprise, the structure of trade union organisation and the average level of education of the employees. While this is an area of growing significance which calls for in-depth research at least on a sample basis, it might be possible, at this stage, to have a brief outlook into the right to strike of workers in public enterprises.

Organised labour resorts to strike action as an ultimate manifestation of the conflicts it may have with an employer or the State. Considering the position of public enterprises as the biggest employers of organised labour, one might tend to believe that the frequency of strikes would be higher in them than in other sectors. In African countries, however, the right to strike, particularly in public enterprises, is subject to many conditions. At the outset, in almost all African countries, public enterprises which are considered essential services are denied the right to strike. Even in public enterprises which are not defined as essential services, strikes are lawful only after the procedures provided in the law for the settlement of disputes have been exhausted. In most African countries, strikes are illegal before a dispute has been submitted for settlement as well as during the actual process of settlement. The procedure for the settlement of disputes mostly ends after a decision is given by a court or an arbitration body; the decisions of these bodies being mostly final and binding. This is the case in a number of countries like Kenya, Malawi, Nigeria, Swaziland, Tanzania, Zambia and in most of the French-speaking African countries. Looking at the chronological sequence of procedures, i.e., prohibition of strike before submission of the dispute, prohibition during settlement of the dispute and, finally, the issue of a binding decision or award, one wonders whether the right to strike actually exists in most African countries. Paradoxically, in spite of the constraints and the rigid procedures to be followed, strikes do take place in African countries, including in public enterprises. It is interesting to note that the frequency of strikes has in some instances increased when there has been firm and complete prohibition. This was, for instance, the case in Nigeria, where the military Government completely banned strikes from 1968 to 1976 for many reasons, including the Civil War and emergency conditions. With such a ban, one would naturally expect that there would at least be a sharp decline in the number of strikes. But this was not so; on the contrary, the number of strikes increased by about three times compared to that in the previous period. In Zambia, which had been known for the infrequency of strikes since 1968, there was a series of strikes by the railway workers in 1978. A strike in Swaziland's paper and pulp company, a major public enterprise in the country, in 1980, is another interesting example.

The crucial issue that arises with respect to strikes in public enterprises in African countries is the finding of a balance between the right to strike, which is a fundamental element for the credibility of the process of collective bargaining, and the urge for rapid economic and social development on the part of the States. It becomes essential to examine to what extent the right to strike can be limited, to understand the causes of strikes and to study the possibilities of creating a healthy atmosphere which guarantees the basic rights to workers but avoids confrontation and waste of resources.

Personnel policies and practices

Personnel policies of public enterprises in African countries are formulated at two different levels. In the first instance, national legislations state broad requirements, mostly in the areas of recruitment, training and wages (minimum wages). On the second level, each public enterprise, depending on its occupational requirements, is to a great extent left on its own to design its policies, especially as they affect administrative organisation, training, motivation, promotion and other related activities directly affecting the worker.

A considerable number of African countries have centralised procedures for recruitment, i.e., an employment and placement office which requires a public enterprise employing above a certain number of workers, and whose operation is expected to last above a certain duration, to notify its existing vacancies; the employment office is then supposed to send possible names of candidates to fill these vacancies. For instance, in Ethiopia, a public enterprise employing more than ten permanent workers and whose operation is expected to last more than three months is obliged to report its vacancies to the Employment Exchange Office, which will immediately provide a list of possible candidates for every post. Sudan has a similar practice, but there are two separate employment exchange offices; one for university graduates and another for other employment seekers. In Zambia, every employer with 25 or more employees must inform the Ministry of Labour of its employment vacancies. Thereupon, candidates for vacant posts are provided by the Ministry. In the Congo all enterprises or establishments are required, by law, to report their vacancies and recruitments of staff to the Employment

Office.[1]   Correspondingly, in Togo, direct recruitment of workers by any kind of enterprise or establishment is prohibited.[2]

As concerns the employment of foreigners, nearly all of the African countries have strict legal requirements and policies to be followed. These usually require that every effort be made, especially in public enterprises, to ascertain that a national who is capable of taking the post should be given the opportunity before a foreigner is considered. If after such a process a foreigner is employed, other legal provisions also require that a national be employed at the same time so that he may serve as a counterpart and take over the job after a given period of time. In Zambia, the Zambianisation Committee, which is composed of representatives of the Government, employers and workers, has the power to investigate any public enterprise with regard to the question of foreign employees and is entitled to review work permits with a view to replacing foreigners by Zambians.

In some countries certain legal provisions also set a number of requirements in the employment and training field. For instance, in the Sudan, the Employers' and Employed Persons Act, 1948 (Amendment 1973), stipulates that written contracts of employment shall not be binding on illiterate persons unless read to them and attested by a responsible person. In Zaire the contract of employment must be submitted to the National Employment Service for endorsement.

As regards personnel management proper, many public enterprises have not yet fully realised the significance of adopting modern policies and practices. Written statements of personnel policy exist only rarely. Even where there are written personnel policies, usually in large public enterprises, they are drawn up by legal advisers and drafted in legalistic language, mainly with the aim of protecting the interests of the public enterprise. Moreover, they are often prepared in a language that the workers do not understand (English or French). In addition, the specialised personnel services that only exist in large-scale public enterprises are not given in many cases enough importance and attention. Advice from personnel departments is often not readily accepted by line managers.

When the programme of Africanisation was launched in many African countries, the personnel department was the first to be Africanised, at least on paper, but either no real training was given to new African personnel managers so as to enable them to fulfil their functions or insufficient authority was given to the posts. As a result, inadequate practices have taken root in some African countries. Some undertakings have been known to practise a certain degree of nepotism because of political considerations or ethnic affiliations. Top-level officials of public enterprises have been appointed on considerations other than merit and this practice seems to have trickled down to the lower levels, sometimes leading to a sort of "spoils system".

---

[1] ILO: Legislative Series, 1964 - Congo (Bra.) 1, Article 163.

[2] ibid., 1975 - Togo 1, Article 161.

The written personnel policies in many African countries, for the most part, seek to promote equitable procedures which take account of the necessary efficiency of public enterprises on the one hand, and give due consideration to such factors as merit and seniority of the personnel on the other. However, these efforts have not always been successful since numbers of public enterprises have been criticised for their inefficiency. In some cases, as in Ghana, Nigeria and Zaire, this has led to the appointment by the Government of certain commissions and consultative bodies to examine and recommend appropriate solutions to remedy these difficulties.

Consultation with trade unions in the formulation of personnel policies is not very common in African countries. However, in certain cases like Egypt, Guinea, Tanzania and Zambia, workers' representatives do, directly or indirectly, participate in committees for recruitment and selection. As mentioned earlier, nearly all French-speaking African countries provide for the election of staff delegates by workers. Under the existing labour codes, the functions of staff delegates include not only presenting workers' grievances but also performing certain personnel tasks such as making suggestions for improving the organisation and output of the undertaking. In some of these countries works committees for co-operation and consultation between workers and management have also been set up.

Generally speaking, the very creation of public enterprises was among other things to make them good examples of personnel practices and other policies in order that the private sector might conform to their standards. This was, for example, the case in Mali where public enterprises were designed to serve as models or examples by their good economic management, the rational use of equipment, strict labour discipline, productivity and profitability.[1] Similarly, in Nigeria public enterprises were, inter alia, expected to establish a set of regulatory devices to make private enterprises conform as much as possible to standards of good practice.[2]

While these were the expectations and objectives of the States, the actual personnel practices in public enterprises have not always been exemplary. Consequently, it would be pertinent to find out why such disparities exist between policies and practices and to try to arrive at some workable remedies and solutions to the shortcomings. In addition, the very concept of public enterprises as "model employers" might be discussed more thoroughly than it has been so far, the main problem being to what extent this concept can be reconciled with the necessary efficiency of public undertakings.

Workers' participation other than collective bargaining

In addition to the process of collective bargaining which may be considered as a form of participation in decision making, other forms of workers' participation in management decisions have been

---

[1] Statut général des entreprises nationales de la République du Mali, Ordonnance du 12.4.69 (JO, 15.4.69).

[2] O. Aboyade, op. cit., p. 33.

attracting some attention in recent years. However, except for a few countries like Algeria, Libya, Madagascar and Tanzania, which have to some extent introduced certain forms of self-management in selected undertakings, mostly public enterprises, those types of workers' participation which have a far-reaching effect in management decisions are hardly practised in African countries. Employers are obviously against such types of workers' participation; nor, paradoxically, have trade unions pressed for their introduction. The lack of keen interest on the part of workers' organisations may be due to the fact that many trade union leaders in these countries feel technically too weak to assume such responsibilities, or it may well be because of fear that traditional trade union functions may be undermined in the process of promoting such workers' participation schemes.

In Algeria, a self-management system was introduced in 1963 in large-scale public enterprises (state-owned, modern agricultural estates). In Libya, the Government has recently established self-management schemes based on the concept of Islamic Socialism, in a substantial part of the public sector. In Tanzania, self-management may be seen in the Ujamaa type of undertakings, and in Madagascar a system which appears to be somewhat in between self-management and worker representation at board level has been introduced in public enterprises (in industry, mines and commerce), under the 1976 Charter of Socialist Undertakings.

Another type of workers' participation limited to public enterprises, i.e. participation in management boards, is practised in a number of African countries, including Benin, Congo, Egypt, Ghana, Libya, Mali, Nigeria, the Sudan and Tanzania. Nevertheless, it should be noted that in these countries, except for Benin and Tanzania, representation in management boards is not provided for on an equal basis. Besides, the scope of the application of the schemes, the manner of appointment of workers' representatives, the role they are expected to play and the influence they may have on decisions vary from one country to another. In Tanzania, for instance, board representation on an equal basis is provided for but elections are conducted along the guidelines given by the ruling political party. In Egypt, Libya and the Sudan, the Government regulates the number of workers' representatives, directly or indirectly influences appointments and determines the duration of service of each representative. The Public Corporation Act of 1976 in the Sudan stipulates that only a limited number of workers' representatives may be included in the boards (usually two); their selection to these positions is very much determined by the Minister. In Nigeria, legal provisions for workers' participation in decision making through management boards apply only to some public enterprises, namely the Nigerian Railway Corporation, the Nigerian Coal Corporation, the Nigerian Port Authority and the Electricity Corporation of Nigeria.

Workers' participation through works councils or works committees is also practised in certain public enterprises of some African countries, including Burundi, Gabon, Mauritania, Mauritius, Tanzania, Tunisia, Zaire and Zambia. In Mauritius the implementation of the system is optional. Works councils in Tanzania and Zambia are composed of two-thirds workers and one-third management. In Tanzania, the chairmanship is given to JUWATA whereas in Zambia, each council is left to draw up its rules and elect its own chairman from among the members.

In other countries such as Ethiopia and Somalia workers' participation is one of the items for bargaining. Employers and trade unions can actually decide around the negotiating table what type of workers' participation they will adopt. In Somalia, the labour laws specifically support workers' participation but do not determine the type or form to be followed.

As can be seen from the above, many forms of workers' participation schemes are practised in public enterprises in many African countries, but the actual outcome of these schemes in terms of labour-management relations and productivity as well as their future trends cannot be easily determined from available data. However, in Africa, where deep-rooted traditions have encouraged joint discussions and consultations, especially by elders, in resolving all social problems, it would appear that labour-management relations in public enterprises would follow these traditions leading to the promotion of workers' participation in management decisions. On the other hand, considering the fact that effective workers' participation will require a relatively high level of education as well as technical skill on the part of the workers and in view of the relatively low status of education, the issue of promoting certain forms of workers' participation in public enterprises remains problematic.

Concluding remarks

A study on labour-management relations in public enterprises in Africa would have been more comprehensive if it had included data on the actual size of public enterprises, on their contribution to GNP and on the labour force they employ. Its usefulness would, moreover, have been enhanced if comparative data between public enterprises and the private sector and the civil service on such items as collective agreements and their application; wages and fringe benefits, cause of labour disputes and frequency of strikes had been given and analysed for different periods. Unfortunately, such data are not easily available. Nevertheless, with available information, some basic inferences have been drawn, and certain fundamental problems and issues with regard to labour-management relations have been raised.

In the last 20 years the size of public enterprises in all of African countries has been constantly increasing. The rate of the increase has varied over the years depending on the socio-economic conditions as well as the political structure and inclination of each country. In a number of countries, such as Botswana, Gabon, Kenya, Liberia, Mauritius, Senegal and Sierra Leone, public enterprises have had a relatively slow but constant pattern of growth. In some others, like Algeria, Ethiopia, Guinea, Libya, Tanzania and Uganda, the pattern of growth has been more pronounced, depending mainly on the political climate prevailing in each of these countries. In a few countries, including Egypt, Ghana and the Sudan, public enterprises initially grew very fast but later slowed down (to some extent reversed), reflecting the liberalised economic policies that were adopted by these countries in 1971, 1966 and 1976 respectively. As a whole, even though the characteristics of growth of each country may be different, public enterprises have been increasing in both size and variety.

Considering that the wage-earning population in African countries is at present very small (in most cases less than 5 per cent of the total population), that there will be a continuous process of industrialisation in the coming years, and that governments are bound to play a leading role in the process of industrialisation, the future growth and expansion of public enterprises seems inevitable.

It is also a fact that industrialisation will entail structural and organisational changes in the relationship between man and his work. The situation where the worker may have one foot in the village and the other in the factory may have to give way to a greater commitment to industrial life and industrial relations. In this connection, two of the important points that have been underlined in the study are that workers in public enterprises have for the most part secured the basic right to organise themselves and that in point of fact public enterprises are, in practically all African countries, the biggest employers of organised labour. However, these two points, although important, are not enough to explain satisfactorily the characteristics of labour-management relations systems and practices in public enterprises.

It has been noted that labour-management relations practices in public enterprises are, in some respects, different from those in the other sectors. These differences are often introduced by governments under various forms resulting from the application of certain legal provisions or based on certain economic and social rationales such as essentiality of services to the community. The central issue in this respect is the acceptable extent of these differences, i.e., the limits within which they are justifiable in terms both of efficient production and the promotion of sound labour-management relations.

In the first place, there appears to be no uniformly applicable definition which would adequately describe public enterprises and delimit them from other sectors of the economy. They have been characterised as having the qualities of the private sector and the accountability of the civil service. But the ideal mixture, where proper control of public funds is exercised and where the freedom of action is permitted in order that the latest techniques of management and market trends can be followed, is not easy to achieve. This is revealed in many African countries, where, on account of political, structural or administrative weaknesses, public enterprises have been incapable of competing with the private sector and rather ended up as partial failures in terms of economic production and services.

On the other hand, workers in public enterprises have in many countries been the founders of trade unionism and many large-scale public enterprises have been among the first to establish proper personnel policies and have pioneered the setting up of some forms of workers' participation schemes. This may lead to the conclusion that public enterprises are model employers and that their labour-management relations practices are exemplary. Yet, in a number of cases the dangers exist of over-centralisation and the erosion of the democratic principles and procedures essential for harmonious industrial relations. In many public enterprises, the right to strike, without which the credibility of the process of collective bargaining is threatened, is very much restricted, if not prohibited. On the part of the management of public enterprises, the autonomy which is necessary for the give and take in collective bargaining is often limited to certain specified areas and major items, such as wages, are sometimes excluded from the bargaining table.

This is not to say that labour-management relations practices in public enterprises in Africa have lost all their voluntaristic features but merely to underline the point that the promotion of sound systems of labour relations in public enterprises will require the striking of a balance between the aims and goals of national economic and social development including accountability for public resources, and the autonomy required by the management to make efficient decisions as well as the safeguarding of the democratic rights of workers.

PART II

NATIONAL MONOGRAPHS

LABOUR MANAGEMENT RELATIONS IN
PUBLIC ENTERPRISES IN AFRICA:
THE NIGERIAN CASE

by

T.M. Yesufu, Ph.D

Human Resources Research Unit,
University of Lagos,
Nigeria

I. General background

There is nothing that has characterised Nigeria's political history in the last 30 years so much as the extention of government influence, intervention and control in almost all aspects of the nation's social and economic life. This has been manifested through the proliferation of institutions acting on behalf of the Government and enjoying varying degrees of autonomy. Separate from the traditional civil service, they nevertheless constitute in general parlance, part of the public service as currently used in Nigeria. Some of these institutions, however, predate the Second World War. And Nigeria's colonial record is surprisingly replete with examples of government involvement in enterprises which, in the erstwhile British capitalist tradition, could have been regarded as outside the purview of public administration - railways, coal exploitation and mineral exploitation; construction and maintenance of ports, harbours and water works; and even stone quarrying, boat building, rice hauling, furniture manufacture, and saw milling.

Most of the non-utilities, such as stone quarrying, and furniture were not very extensive; modest in size, they were designed essentially to supply the needs of the Government itself. Accordingly, as Aboyade put it, "the hey-days for the establishment and expansion of public enterprises in Nigeria was the period between the end of the Second World War and the achievement of political independence".[1] There was an even more rapid proliferation of public enterprises after the inception of military rule as the country was transformed from a federation of four regions into one, first of 12 States, and then, 19 States. Each new State has not only inherited some public enterprise institutions from its parent region or state, but has in most cases created new ones. Nowhere, however, is the term public enterprise legally defined.

The Nigerian Constitution defines public service to include the traditional civil service and certain other enumerated bodies. Some of the public enterprises, such as the broadcasting corporations and universities, are by that definition part of the public service, but others such as some commercial banks in which the Government has controlling interests, are excluded. The essence of public enterprises in Nigeria, therefore, is not whether they are part of the public service or not, but that they are nevertheless distinguishable by certain well-defined characteristics. For the purpose of this paper we may define public enterprises in Nigeria as those institutions not being part of the civil service (ministries and extra-ministerial departments), in which the Government has controlling interest and which are specifically designed as instruments for promoting or sustaining economic and social development.

The rationale for the development of public enterprises in Nigeria is the same as in all mixed economies with a strong bias towards private capitalism. In essence, the role of the public sector in national development is summarised as:

---

[1] O. Aboyade: *Nigerian Public Enterprises as an Organisational Dilemma, Public Enterprises in Nigeria* (Nigerian Economic Society, 1973), p. 30.

[2] ibid.

(a) providing the necessary infrastructural facilities for private enterprise to operate;

(b) establishing a set of regulatory devices to make private enterprise conform as much as possible to standards of good behaviour; and

(c) supplementing private enterprise investment activity where this is not forthcoming adequately or promptly.[1]

The civil service, through the national development plans, ministerial and departmental regulations, by-laws, etc., supplemented by central bank regulations, normally performs the functions in item (b), but the public enterprises, with which we are here concerned, are the main instruments for effecting items (b) and (c). It is the case, therefore, that the philosophical or ideological standpoint which would restrict public enterprise to mere provision of public utilities and the minimum of basic infrastructures, never found firm root in Nigeria and, from the tentative beginnings of the colonial era, Nigerian governments have come to participate in a massive way in all aspects of national development. Thus, "broadly speaking, it is to public enterprise that is assigned the greater part of the task of laying the basis upon which the structure of a dynamic and diversified economy is to arise. Prominent among its functions is the provision of power and transport. Equally, is the improvement of agricultural productivity, through irrigation schemes, fertilizer factories, credit institutions, marketing boards, etc. ... Upon the competence with which the State copes with these heavy tasks depends the whole economic future of the country, whatever may be the terms in which that future is conceived".[2]

While the role which public enterprises play is clear and is generally agreed, the reasons for creating them independently of the civil service have not always met with uncritical acceptance. The main reason generally advanced for their creation is that the enterprises concerned are required to undertake services or economic activities where speed of decision making, risk taking and processes are such that they cannot be effectively administered through the normal civil service machinery - a machinery that is perforce characterised by caution, political interference, undue publicity, etc.

Rejecting a suggestion that public enterprises be brought directly under the civil service, a government working party concluded that, "the complexities of modern administration are such that the Government should, in its own interest, operate directly within a limited field, and should devise a machinery whereby its undertakings of a large-scale commercial and public utility character could operate with some measure of autonomy but under its general surveillance. Since public corporations and state-owned companies provide such a machinery they must be retained, and we would not therefore subscribe to any recommendation that they should

---

[1] Aboyade: op. cit., p. 33.

[2] A.H. Hanson: Public Enterprise and Economic Development (Routledge and Kegan Paul, Ltd., London, 1959), p. 182.

either be scrapped or be translated to government departments".[1] Thus, considerations of efficiency deriving from division of labour have also been advanced to underpin the creation of public enterprises.

The need for freedom from political interference has also sometimes been stressed. As the same working party put it, "the purpose of setting up public corporations is to enable certain state enterprises, while still responsible to the Government, to operate as commercial concerns and be able to pay their way, meet their capital charges and if possible, make profits ... Another fundamental point", continued the committee, "is that if public corporations are to operate as commercial concerns, they cannot do so successfully unless their policies are guided by commercial considerations. They must therefore be secured freedom from party politics".[2] In some cases, and particularly since the highly inflationary market forces that have marked the years since the civil war, the Government has felt constrained to set up some public institutions - such as the National Supply Company - to safeguard the interests of the consumer against the exploiting propensities of private monopolies in a market that seemed to have virtually transformed into a sellers' haven.

Just as the reasons for establishing public enterprises vary, so also do their structure, organisation, methods and control. This is not surprising considering their scope, which span, as we have seen, the terrains of public utilities, transportation, manufacturing, distribution, services such as banking, education, etc. Historically, the first public enterprises such as railways, harbours and ports, electricity, and coalmining, were run as government departments between the two world wars. They were translated into public corporations of the British prototype in the early 1950s - the Nigerian Railway Corporation, the Nigerian Ports Authority, the Nigerian Coal Corporation, the Electricity Corporation of Nigeria (now Nigerian Electric Power Authority). The post-Second World War period also saw the establishment of a number of produce marketing boards. With the federalisation of the Constitution in the 1950s, the second half of that decade witnessed the growth of many more boards and corporations established by the regional governments, ostensibly to promote development within their areas. The marketing boards and development corporations were products of this era.

The governments began also to take direct interest in econonic activities _per se_. They established farm settlements, rubber, oil palm and other plantations. The 1960s saw the competitive entry by the governments into the textile industry, cement production, soft drinks and beer brewing, while the federal Government set up a distillery in Lagos and a national shipping company. After Ghana's independence in 1957, its ultra-nationalist approach to its relations with its neighbours led to the break up of the West African Airways Corporation and the West African Currency Board, and the Nigerian Government felt constrained to create in their place its own Nigeria Airways Corporation and the Nigerian Security Printing and Minting Company.

---

[1] _Report of the Working Party on Statutory Corporations and State-owned Companies_ (Federal Ministry of Information, Lagos, 1966), para. 7, p. 8.

[2] ibid., para. 8, p. 9.

After the civil war the 12 States created in 1967 from the previous four regions embarked on a course of aggressive intervention in economic development under the direction of military governors. They entered the fields of road transportation, residential building construction, etc., in a big way, in direct competition with private enterprise. In the case of river transportation, some of the States bordering the River Niger and its delta areas formed a joint enterprise. Rural electricity, water, and other boards, proliferated. One State Government even started a laundry service and several entered the field of supermarket. The explosion in the demand for education led to the establishment of state education boards. By 1970 there were six university institutions, but in 1976 the Federal Military Government created seven more, bringing the total to 13.

The Federal Government in the Third Development Plan, emphasised the policy of indigenising the economy, following which it acquired controlling interest in some erstwhile multinational commercial banks, building societies and oil companies, which in effect became public enterprises. Following public probes into the assets of former public officers at various times, some governments seized some companies from some of the persons concerned, which were promptly converted into government enterprises.

The manner in which public enterprises in Nigeria came into being is, therefore, also as varied as their character. Some, such as the early public corporations - railways, ports, electricity, coal - were created out of government departments. Others such as the Nigerian Airways Corporation were creatures necessitated by international considerations following a break up of a multinational organisation. Some were acquired by mere subcription of controlling shares by the Government in companies that were formerly completely private enterprises, or, indeed, by completely buying out the former owners.

No census of public enterprises in Nigeria exists and even figures of a few years back would be misleading because of the fluid and rapidly changing situation. But an estimate of about 250 which the present writer has made in consultation with various persons would appear to be incomplete, taking federal and state institutions together. They span the whole field of national economic and social endeavour. An interpretation as to their relative importance or predominance by sectors is, accordingly, a difficult matter. Certain areas have come to be reserved completely or almost exclusively for public enterprise - e.g., railways, public electricity and water supply, and air transportation.[1] Apart from these infrastructural and general utilities, public enterprises operate alongside private enterprises - for example, in road transportation, commercial banking, manufacturing (textiles, breweries, etc.). In some cases, while the physical presence of public enterprise may be minor, its influence and impact could be tremendous. This has been the case in the distributive trade, where massive importation and distribution of scarce food items, such as rice, flour, sugar and meat, have tended to keep the rate of inflation in some check.

---

[1] Even in some of these fields the public monopoly is tempered, however slightly. For example, a private electricity company still operates near Jos, and private air charter companies are in existence although they cannot compete with the Nigeria Airways for public passenger traffic within the country.

In some fields of manufacturing and commerce, the Government felt the need to step in partly to fill some vacuum where private enterprises have shown inadequate interest, and partly to temper or even break the monopolistic effect of certain private sector operations. The education sector is now completely taken over by the governments as a matter of public policy and the pioneering and development work of the missionaries and even private philanthropic or profit-seeking entrepreneurs has been taken over by the federal and state governments. While the universities operate under their own statutes, the secondary and primary schools are placed for the most part under state school boards or boards of education.

As one might expect, these multifarious enterprises operate, as already indicated, with varying degrees of autonomy. In theory only important policy matters are reserved for the Government, while day-to-day administration and methods devolve on the boards of these enterprises. This tends to approximate to the actual practice, however, only in a few cases, and the principle, under the former civilian governments, was honoured almost invariably in the breach.[1] The Federal Military Government, following a recommendation of the Working Party on Statutory Corporations, decided to re-establish the principle, condemned government and ministerial interference in the day-to-day administration of public enterprises and corporations, and reformulated the necessary safeguards.[2]

Experience has shown, however, that it is even more difficult for public enterprises to exercise autonomy under military rule than under civilian governments. The education and school boards tend to operate almost directly under the surveillance and control of the Ministries of Education. Some state-owned newspapers seem to work (in spite of all protestations to the contrary) under the umbrella of "unofficial" censorship. Even industrial concerns such as cement works, breweries and textile mills, tend to suffer undue interference because of the pressures on the governments concerned, by vested interests. However, some enterprises such as the railways, coal, and the National Electric Power Authority (NEPA), seem to have been able to operate with some credible degree of autonomy in their day-to-day administration. But the whole issue of the relations between the public enterprises and their sponsoring governments is one which is bound to arise again soon after the return to civilian rule.

In terms of wage employment the public sector has traditionally been dominant in the Nigerian economy. In 1975 it accounted for 65 per cent or 1 million, of the total modern sector employment of 1.75 million. The public corporations and boards accounted for 16 per cent of total public sector employment and the teaching services for 19 per cent. Public enterprises as herein defined, therefore, accounted for 35 per cent of public sector employment, giving a public services employment figure of about 350,000 in that year.[3]

---

[1] Report of the Working Party, op. cit., pp. 8-11.

[2] The Policy of the Federal Military Government on Statutory Corporations and State-owned Companies (Federal Ministry of Information, 1968), paras. 6-11.

[3] T.M. Yesufu: The Dynamics of Industrial Relations: The Nigerian Experience (Oxford University Press, forthcoming early 1979), Chapter II. See also Third National Development Plan, 1975-80, table 32.4, p. 37.

II. Characteristics of labour-management relations in public enterprises

In general, labour policy in Nigeria made no distinction between public enterprises and other sectors of the economy, until very recently. That policy was evolved along the inherited British tradition under which labour-management relations, whether in public or private enterprises, rely heavily upon free collective bargaining. Up to the advent of military rule in 1966, public conern was to make that policy effective through the development of legislation that would promote the requisite trade unions and employers' organisations, to facilitate collective bargaining, and to establish machinery for the apprehension and settlement of trade disputes. The trade union legislation was of general application, and the general machinery for settlement of disputes - in the form of conciliation, mediation, or arbitration - was both "ad hoc" and voluntary. The recent departure from the erstwhile system has been not so much a change in policy, but a tightening up of the trade union law, and the institutionalisation of the machinery for dealing with industrial disputes. In the process, the public services - including the public enterprises as here defined - have come in for special mention, consideration and treatment. This section will highlight these special areas relating to public enterprises within the general policy and legal framework as exist at present.

The legal framework

Legislation as it relates to labour-management relations normally reflects existing labour policy. In this respect, Nigeria's traditional policy of industrial democracy was rather dented during the civil war (1967-70), and during the following period of national emergency which was only recently lifted in 1978. For example, "Government felt compelled to ban strikes and lockouts and, as a means of controlling inflation, decided to limit the freedom of employers and workers to negotiate increases in wages. With the continuation of emergency even after the civil war, restriction of collective bargaining and, therefore, industrial democracy was maintained".[1] Following the decision to return the country to civil rule by 1979, the Government in 1975 reviewed, among other things, its labour policy. The Federal Commissioner of Labour announced that the Federal Military Government had "decided on a new national labour policy which will involve limited government intervention in certain areas of labour activity in order to ensure industrial peace, progress and harmony", and the Government would be "pursuing the policy of guided democracy in labour matters. This policy", the Commissioner elaborated, "is predicated on the continued guarantee of freedom of association, the promotion of strong, stable and responsible workers' and employers' organisations, the establishment and development of a suitable institutional framework for the effective prevention and expeditious settlement of labour disputes, the promotion of labour-management co-operation and of consultation at appropriate levels between workers, employers and government, and the vigorous enforcement of the provisions of

---

[1] T.M. Yesufu: The Dynamics of Industrial Relations, op. cit., Chapter III.

labour legislation relating to minimum conditions of employment, social security, safety, health and welfare at work".[1]

As stated, there seemed to be hardly anything new as compared with the long-established policy of industrial democracy and minimum state intervention. While ostensibly pursuing the same objectives, however, the implementation has displayed, in practice, greater government intervention in industrial relations and a restriction of voluntarism on the part of workers and employers with regard to the formation, administration, and operation of trade unions, and the use of institutions for the settlement of industrial disputes. Thus, the new trade union legislation still provides in theory for freedom of workers or employers to join or organise trade unions. But it goes further to reorganise and restructure the trade unions into 70 industrial unions (46 of them workers' organisations); and a worker can only belong (or decline to belong) to the union stipulated by law to cater for his class of employment. An application for registration of a new trade union can only be considered in respect of workers or employers where a trade union does not already exist - a very unlikely possibility, in view of the industrial scope of the statutory unions. Check-off, as a means of paying union dues is now legally compulsory - although the right of a worker to contract out in writing is guaranteed. Freedom to form central trade unions has also been removed and only one central labour organisation - the Nigeria Labour Congress - is established and recognised by law. And it is now compulsory for an employer to recognise a registered trade union.[2]

Prior to military rule, the conduct of day-to-day relations between management and labour was, in theory and practice, truly voluntary. Joint consultation and collective bargaining machinery were only established and used by mutual agreement, and to the extent agreed, between the parties concerned. In cases of breakdown in relations, resulting in trade disputes, resort could be had to the provisions of the Trade Disputes (Arbitration and Inquiry) Ordinance, 1941. But, under that law, conciliation, mediation and arbitration were almost completely dependent upon the will and voluntary acceptance of the parties, and collective agreements were not legally enforceable.

During the civil war, the Trade Disputes (Emergency Provisions) (Amendment) Decree No. 21 of 1968 was enacted, and subsequently amended by the Trade Disputes (Emergency Provisions) (Amendment) (No. 2) Decree No. 53 of 1969. These decrees banned strikes and introduced provisions for compulsory arbitration, and under Decree No. 53 of 1969, an Industrial Arbitration Tribunal was established. These earlier decrees were superseded by the Trade Disputes Decree No. 7 of 1976, which made fresh provisions with respect to the settlement of trade disputes. While directing that efforts to settle a trade dispute must first be attempted by negotiation by the parties concerned, the Decree makes provisions for compulsory conciliation and arbitration as the Commissioner for Labour may

---

[1] Address by Brigadier Henry E.O. Adefope, Commissioner for Labour, to Representatives of the Four Central Labour Organisations and the Nigeria Employers Consultative Association on the New National Policy on Labour at a meeting held in the Senate Chamber on Thursday, 4 December 1975.

[2] The Trade Unions Decree No. 31 of 1973, as amended by the Trade Unions (Amendment) Decree No. 22 of 1978.

decide. The awards of an Arbitration Tribunal once confirmed by the Commissioner, are binding, as are the agreements reached through conciliation. Where there is objection, the Commissioner refers the matter to the Industrial Court, which also has powers to pronounce on the interpretation of collective agreements. The decision of the Industrial Court is final and binding on all the parties concerned.

The 1976 Decree also prohibits strikes where the laid down procedures for resolving disputes have not been exhausted or where the Industrial Court has issued an award. "This in effect means that once a dispute has started to follow the normal course, strikes are legally forbidden in Nigeria. It constitutes a fundamental departure from the former principle of freedom to strike under the inherited British traditional system of free collective bargaining."[1]

The Trade Disputes (Essential Services) Decree No. 23 of 1976, amended Decree No. 7 of 1976 in fundamental respects. Thus, Decree No. 23 of 1976 empowers the Commissioner for Labour to refer a dispute in an essential service compulsorily to arbitration whether or not the dispute has been formally notified to him. It unequivocally bans strikes and lockouts in the essential services as defined in the law. It empowers the Government to proscribe any trade union or association of persons employed in an essential service if the Government is satisfied that the union or association has engaged in acts to cause industrial unrest or to disrupt the smooth running of the enterprise. And it confers powers also on the Inspector-General of Police, and the Chief of Staff, Supreme Military Headquarters, to order the detention of any official or member of a proscribed organisation who, subsequent to being proscribed, engages in acts calculated to cause industrial unrest.

These provisions are of general application and apply, accordingly, to public as well as other enterprises. However, the effect of some sections of the Trade Unions Decree and the Trade Disputes (Essential Services) Decree is such as to place large sections of the public service, including public enterprises, in a special category in law and in the conduct of labour-management relations. We shall return to these issues subsequently.

Apart from these basic provisions of the law which apply to all employments, each of the public corporations and boards, which constitute the public enterprises, is normally set up under its own enabling legislation, by the Federal or State Government as the case may be. Generally, the regulation of relations with, and the terms and conditions of the employment of, employees is placed within the competence of the respective governing board. In 1968 the Federal Military Government, after considering the report of the Working Party on Statutory Corporations, accepted the latter's recommendation for a machinery to regulate and set uniform terms and conditions of service for the corporations and state-owned companies.[2] And for the purpose, it established a

---

[1] T.M. Yesufu: <u>The Dynamics of Industrial Relations</u>, op. cit.

[2] <u>The Policy of the Federal Military Government on Statutory Corporations and State-owned Companies</u> (Federal Ministry of Information, 1968), op. cit., para. 33.

Statutory Corporations Service Commission by Decree No. 53 of 1968.[1] That Decree was supplemented by the Statutory Corporations (Salaries and Allowances, etc.) Decree No. 59 of 1968, which established uniform salary scales for the public enterprises concerned.

The above laws, however, applied to federal public enterprises, but as could be expected under a military regime, the state governments soon followed the lead of the Federal Military Government in practice, if not by law. This centralisation of the machinery for regulating the terms and conditions of service for public enterprises has had important consequences for their labour-management relations, to which we shall return.

Trade unions and employers' organisations

Trade union legislation is of general application to both workers' and employers' organisations. Thus, the extant legislation, the Trade Unions Decree, 1973, defines a trade union as, "any combination of workers or employers, whether temporary or permanent, the purpose of which is to regulate the terms and conditions of employment of workers, whether the combination in question would or would not, apart from this Decree, be an unlawful combination by reason of any of its purposes being in restraint of trade, and whether its purposes do or do not include the provisions of benefits for its members". However, whereas not less than 50 workers are required to subscribe to the application for registration of a trade union, only two employers may apply for registration. For the purpose of the law, a worker is defined by the Trade Unions Decree as "any employee, that is to say, any member of the public service of the federation or of a state or any individual (other than a member of any such public service) who has entered into or worked under a contract with an employer, whether the contract is for manual labour, clerical work or otherwise, expressed or implied, oral or in writing, and whether it is a contract personally to execute any work or labour or a contract of apprenticeship".

It is clear from the foregoing that workers in public enterprises, like their colleagues in the other arms of the public service or in private enterprises, can in law, organise trade unions. However, the Trade Unions Decree specifically bars certain classes of employees from organising or belonging to a trade union, some of which constitute public enterprises as covered in this paper. These are the Security Printing and Minting Company Limited, and the Nigerian External Telecommunications Limited.[2] The fact that they were listed along with the military establishments (army, navy, air force), the police, prisons, the central bank, and the customs preventive services, indicates that the two enterprises concerned are considered to be of special importance in the security system of the country.

Thus, workers in public enterprises, except the two above-mentioned, can organise or join trade unions on the same terms and conditions as workers in other forms of enterprise. However, the

---

[1] The Statutory Corporations Service Commission Decree No. 53 of 1968.

[2] The Trade Unions Decree, 1973, section 11.

country frowned at the multiplicity of trade unions which resulted from the liberal provisions of the Trade Unions Ordinance, 1938. That law was superseded by the Trade Unions Decree No. 31 of 1973 which, as amended by the Trade Unions (Amendment) Decree No. 22 of 1978, restructured the erstwhile previously existing 1,000 odd trade unions, along industrial lines and reduced their number to 70, including employers' organisations and senior staff associations. Of the number, 46 are, as already indicated, trade unions of workers.[1] The unions thus cut across the barriers of individual establishments, enterprises or firms. Therefore, not only can workers in public enterprises belong to the same unions as other workers, they have in many cases been compulsorily grouped along with them. Thus, the Nigerian Union of Journalists includes workers in state and federal newspaper enterprises as well as their colleagues in the privately owned enterprises. Other examples are the Printing and Publishing Workers' Union, the National Union of Hotel and Personal Service Workers, and the National Union of Electricity and Gas Workers. But in some cases particular classes of employees of some public enterprises are grouped into their own unions; the Academic Staff Union of Universities, the Nigerian Ports Authority Workers' Union, the Nigerian Coal Miners Union are examples. They are exclusive, however, only by reference to the nature of their work, and not as a matter of policy, deriving from their status as public enterprises. Thus, the multiplicity and mixed grill of industrial, craft, house, and general unions in Nigeria have been superseded, through deliberate policy, reflected in law, by industrial unions - however imperfectly the statutory groupings turned out to have been.

While membership of trade Unions remains ostensibly voluntary under the law, the effect of the Trade Unions (Amendment) Decree, 1976, if read along with the Labour (Amendment) Decree No. 21 of 1978, is to make membership of trade unions compulsory for all workers eligible to join or organise unions. Thus, the latter Decree, amending subsection 3 of section 5 of the Labour Decree No. 21 of 1974, provides that upon the registration and recognition of a trade union, the employer is obliged to "make deductions from the wages of all workers eligible to be members of the union for the purpose of paying contributions to the trade union so recognised", and pay the sums so deducted to the union. But the Trade Unions (Amendment) Decree, 1978, stipulates that all the unions listed thereunder, which cover virtually all industries and employees, shall be deemed to be registered, and makes their recognition by employers mandatory. It is true that the Labour (Amendment) Decree, 1978, provides that a worker may contract out of the system in writing. Experience shows, however, that it is very difficult and always impolitic in practice for the worker to exercise this right. In Nigeria, most workers are in fact ignorant of this right and there is no information that any significant number has exercised it. It follows that in public enterprises as in other employments, recent legislation has made unionisation of the relevant employees, virtually complete.

As already indicated, the Trade Unions (Amendment) Decree, 1978, made provision for only one central labour organisation - the Nigeria Labour Congress (NLC). Trade unions embracing employees in public enterprises are, along with all other trade unions, affiliated by law to the NLC as full-fledged members.

---

[1] The Trade Unions (Amendment) Decree, No. 22 of 1978, Schedule 3.

They have no disabilities or special status within the movement and, in the national Industrial union as in the NLC, workers of public enterprises can play a role and participate to the same extent as other unions or workers. There is no necessary bond of fellowship or common cause currently discernible among trade unions in public enterprises vis-à-vis other unions, and their influence at the national level must depend to a large extent upon the calibre of their officials and other leaders.

Of the 70 unions stipulated under the Trade Unions (Amendment) Decree, 1978, only nine are organisations of employers. These are in the fields of agriculture; banks and financial institutions; food, beverages and tobacco; hotel and personal services; construction and civil engineering; road transport; mining; and conservancy. These cover only a minority of the enterprises in the public sector, which therefore are still not formally organised under the trade union law. Nevertheless, the new unionism, as spelt out under the Trade Unions Decree, has thrown a new challenge to the Nigeria Employers Consultative Association (NECA) which has redoubled its efforts to organise employers into trade groups. Public enterprises are free to belong to NECA or its affiliated trade groups and some do belong. However, some, particularly those responsible for public utilities which have no counterpart in the private sector, hardly see any reason to join NECA or other trade associations of employers. Where they join they often do so as associates rather than full-fledged members.

Trade union recognition

Since public enterprises do not enjoy any special status under Nigeria's labour law and industrial relations system, it is understandable that no particular legal provisions exist for the recognition of trade unions in these enterprises. Until recently, the recognition of trade unions registered under the Trade Unions Ordinance, 1938, was a voluntary matter between the union and its corresponding management. One of the effects of the liberal provisions of that law was the proliferation of trade unions, even within single enterprises. Some enterprises - particularly in the private sector - exercised their discretion not to recognise a trade union; when this happened the matter was usually settled either by negotiation, conciliation or strike. Following the colonial government's tradition, however, it was unusual for any public enterprise to refuse to recognise a trade union of its employees. But in some cases the trade unions themselves made the conferment of recognition difficult. For example, the Nigerian Railway Corporation had a history of trade union proliferation. From the one Railway Workers' Union formed in 1931, the railways was by the 1970s afflicted by as many as 12 unions, many of them coming into being through internal dissention and internecine strife. In such cases, the management sometimes felt constrained to withhold recognition, not only of a new breakaway union, but of its parent organisation, until the position was clarified. The Corporation ultimately recognised no less than eight unions and dealt with them on behalf of their respective members. A federation - the Nigeria Union of Railwaymen (Federated) was, however, formed, which negotiated with management on matters affecting the generality of the workers.

As already indicated; the Trade Unions Decree, 1973, as amended by the Trade Unions (Amendment) Decree No. 22 of 1978, has changed the situation radically. Most workers of every organisation are grouped into one union, although in some cases the workers, classified into two or three categories, belong to different unions. By reference to Schedule 3 of the Trade Unions (Amendment) Decree No. 22 of 1978, all railway workers now presumably belong only to the Nigeria Union of Railwaymen; so also do the miners of the Nigeria Coal Corporation belong to the Nigerian Coal Miners Union, and the workers of the NPA are now all grouped into the Nigeria Ports Authority Workers' Union. On the other hand, as we have already pointed out, workers of many public enterprises are grouped with their counterparts in the private sector into single industrial unions. This is the case, for example, with respect to employees of the Nigeria National Shipping Line who are covered by the Nigeria Union of Seamen and Water Transport Workers.

With the historical tradition of generous recognition of the past, the workers of public enterprises who are grouped into their own separate individual unions - railways, ports, coal - would have had no problem of recognition under the new dispensation. Indeed, available evidence suggests that the managements welcome the release from the harassment of many unions, and the opportunity to deal with only one or two on behalf of all employees. On the other hand, recognition by a public enterprise of a union embracing employees in the private sector would have been much more difficult. Discretion, however, was removed from management in this matter by the Trade Unions (Amendment) Decree, 1978, which provides that "where there is a trade union of which persons in the employment of an employer are members, that trade union shall, without further assurance, on registration in accordance with the provisions of this Decree, be entitled to recognition by the employer", and further, that, "if an employer deliberately fails to recognise any trade union registered pursuant to the provisions of subsection (1) of this section, he shall be guilty of an offence and be liable on summary conviction to a fine of ₦1,000".

Thus, all that is required for a trade union to obtain recognition from an employer is evidence of registration and indication that some workers of that establishment or enterprise belong to the union. These provisions apply to public enterprises as well as to others, and have the effect of minimising, if not altogether abolishing, recognition disputes. The problems which arise, as is already being witnessed in some enterprises (universities, for example), will be where rival unions claim the membership of the same class of employees, and not from any discretion of the management of a public enterprise to recognise or not to recognise the unions. The law as it stands, makes no special provision for resolving such conflicts and they can, therefore, only be dealt with through the normal machinery of conciliation, mediation or arbitration - albeit between the rival unions concerned. It is a field in which the Nigerian Labour Congress (NLC) is likely to wield important influence. Nevertheless, where the problem is one between the union and the employer, and they are unable to reach agreement, the Commissioner for Labour has powers under the Trade Unions Decree, 1973, to issue an order compelling the employer to recognise the union.

There are no special legal provisions or practices in public enterprises with regard to bargaining bodies or procedures. The general provisions contained in the Trade Disputes Decree No. 21 of 1968 therefore apply to public enterprises. Under the Decree, when a trade dispute arises, the parties concerned must first make effort to resolve it at a meeting between the parties themselves, under the chairmanship of a mediator appointed by them or with their agreement, "thus reaffirming the voluntary negotiation principle in Nigeria's industrial relations system".[1] If within 14 days no agreement is reached at that stage, the matter is reported to the Commissioner for Labour who appoints a conciliator to endeavour by negotiation with the parties to reach a settlement. If within 14 days the conciliator is unable to resolve the dispute, he reports to the Commissioner who, within another 14 days, must refer the matter to the Industrial Arbitration Panel which appoints an Arbitration Tribunal to deal with the dispute. The Tribunal must report on a dispute within 42 days, to the Commissioner for Labour, who publishes it in the Gazette and allows 21 days for any objections thereto. If no objections are raised, the Commissioner confirms the Tribunal's award which then becomes binding on the parties to the dispute. If objections are raised, the Commissioner refers the issue to the Industrial Court whose decision is final and binding.

It is worth noting that collective bargaining need not be undertaken only by a trade union on behalf of workers. The Trade Unions Decree which bans unionism in some enterprises, nevertheless permits the setting up of joint consultative committees through which the workers and management can bargain on any matter relating to terms and conditions of service. While the law is silent on the matter, it does appear that disagreements in such cases can be handled in accordance with the procedures outlined above.

Some of the older public enterprises like the railways, ports, coal and airways, have a long tradition of concluding collective agreements with their workers. Some others, mainly at the state level, have been notorious for indifferent relations with their employees. Until 1968, agreements concluded by the public enterprises included clauses on wages, hours of work, shift, clothing and tool allowances, bonuses of all types, transport and housing allowances, etc. In that year, however, as we have already pointed out, the Federal Military Government legislated against each enterprise having to determine its rates of remuneration and conditions of service, and the Statutory Corporations Service Commission was set up. In that year also the Government decreed against any employer in the country negotiating general increases in wages with workers without reference to the Government. In fact, virtually all negotiated increases of a general nature have been disapproved by the Government, and only such increases as were agreed, following the Adebo and Udoji Wages and Salaries Review Commissions, 1971 and 1974 respectively, have been implemented. The 1968 Decree on statutory corporations, as we have seen, also declared that terms and conditions of service in public enterprises will be on the lines applicable to the rest of the public service. The scope of independent collective bargaining within the public enterprises, therefore, has been effectively limited since then to domestic issues such as increments, methods of pay, shift work, promotions, both at the plant and national levels, as appropriate. It is unlikely that this situation can be long sustained under civilian rule which is expected in 1979. The stronger "industrial" unions which now exist are likely to be much more restive than they currently are under military rule, and would demand scope for the exercise of their legal powers to negotiate any aspect of the terms and conditions of employment, including wages. As things stand,

---

[1] T.M. Yesufu: The Dynamics of Industrial Relations, op. cit.

the Government has pre-empted the sole right to determine the level of wages and salaries and other conditions of service, not only with respect to statutory corporations, but for the whole public service; and severely restricts the movement of wages even in the private sector. There is little or no consultation with workers on these issues, although trade unions can present their cases to the wages commissions that are appointed at rather long intervals.

There are no data from which the impact of collective agreements in public enterprises can be decoded. Normally, such impact is reflected in levels of efficiency and productivity, the state of job satisfaction of the employees, rates of labour turnover, costs of production, and levels of profitability. Over the years, the record of performance of public enterprises in these and other respects has not been impressive in Nigeria. As Aboyade points out, theirs has been a sorry story of disillusionment, and "whatever the laudable aim and however high the hopes at initiation, one after another the Nigerian enterprises have performed over the last two decades in a way that can only be described in polite language as disappointing".[1] These failures, however, could not be attributed primarily or even substantially to the effects of bad labour-management relations in general or to negotiated agreements between both parties in particular. Inept management, ineffective capitalisation, bribery, nepotism and undue political interference have all been contributory. Currently, however, there is manifest a very high rate of labour turnover, very low levels of efficiency and productivity, and low morale in the public services of Nigeria, including the public enterprises. Their wages and salaries have become extremely depressed by reference to the private sector, and it is believed that the situation can be improved, at least partly, by permitting the respective management and workers to negotiate their terms and conditions of employment. With everyone aware that the real authority over these issues lies elsewhere, collective bargaining in public enterprises has become rather impotent and has little influence either on the issues in which the workers themselves are most basically interested, or on other enterprises in the private or public sector.

Labour disputes

By reference to the nature of the labour and industrial relations laws enacted after the inception of military rule in Nigeria in 1966, one would expect to see a serious decline in the number and intensity of labour disputes. For example, from 1968 to 1976 strikes were completely banned in Nigeria, ostensibly because of civil war and emergency conditions. Under the provisions of the Trade Disputes Decree No. 7 of 1976, strikes are prohibited once a dispute is submitted to the normal machinery provided for settlement, until it reaches the Industrial Court, and once the Court makes a pronouncement, its order is final and binding. Even more significantly for public enterprises, the Trade Disputes Decree No. 7 of 1976 as supplemented by the Trade Disputes (Essential Services) Decree No. 23 of 1976, altogether bans strikes and lockouts in the designated essential services of the nation. For the purposes of the Decree "essential services" include, among others:

---

[1] O. Aboyade, op. cit., p. 31.

(a) the federal and state public services including civilian employees of the armed forces who are engaged in any industry or undertaking connected with the manufacture or production of materials for the armed forces;

(b) establishments connected with the supply of electricity, power, water, or fuel of any kind; broadcasting, postal, telegraphic, cable, wireless or telephone communications, ports, harbours, docks or aerodromes, the transportation of persons, goods or livestock whether by road, rail, sea, river or air; burial of the dead, hospitals, treatment of the sick, prevention of diseases and other public health matters including sanitation, road cleaning, disposal of night-soil and rubbish; outbreaks of fire;

(c) banking services, including the central bank, and the Nigeria Security Printing and Minting Company.

It is estimated that "the inclusion of banking services, security printing and minting as well as the public services of the Federation and of the States as essential services, does mean in effect that about 60 per cent of wage earners in Nigeria can no longer lawfully exercise the strike weapon".[1]

Thus, it is ostensibly illegal for employees in the vast majority of public enterprises in Nigeria to go on strike as a means of prosecuting a trade dispute. The only exceptions indeed would appear to be the purely commercial enterprises, like state-owned breweries, textile mills, supermarkets, cinemas, etc. Yet it is one of the great ironies of the military era in Nigeria that, in spite of the decrees aforementioned, the propensity to strike and the intensity of strikes have tended to increase in public enterprises as in other sectors of the economy. For example, in the period 1956 to 1967 for which data are available before the advent of the military regime and the ban on strikes, the highest number of disputes reported in any one year (1960-61) was 140, of which 65 or 46 per cent result in strike action with a loss of 157,373 man-days. Since 1966 when the military came into power, the average number of strikes recorded annually has exceeded 200. In 1971, as many as 501 trade disputes were recorded of which 153 or 31 per cent resulted in strikes with a loss of 209,294 man-days.[2] The conclusion from available data is that, whatever their limitations, "they certainly lend support to the view that, taking one year with another, the state of industrial relations in Nigeria has tended to worsen".[3]

So far as the position of public enterprises is connected, the table annexed to this paper depicts the state of labour-management relations as reflected by the number of recorded trade disputes, strikes and loss of man-days. The data for the education sector and the parastatals represent the position of the public enterprises, with which we are here concerned. The case of the education services sector is very significant. From its formation

---

[1] T.M. Yesufu: op. cit.

[2] T.M. Yesufu: The Dynamics of Industrial Relations, op. cit., tables IX.1 and IX.2.

[3] ibid.

in 1931 until the advent of military rule in 1966, and the banning of strikes in 1968, the Nigerian Union of Teachers was noted for its maturity of approach in matters of industrial relations, and never once called an official strike. Yet the data in the annexed table show that disputes and strikes have become a regular occurrence in the education sector - i.e. among teachers. We have shown in section I of this paper that employment in the education sector constitutes 9 per cent of total public sector employment. But for the three years covered in the annexed table, education accounted for between 21 and 30 per cent of the number of disputes resulting in strikes, and for up to 74 per cent of the man-days lost in the public sector in 1977-78. The figures for the rest of the public enterprises, namely, parastatals (or public corporations) are low by reference to the position in the private sector, but they cannot be regarded as particularly reassuring in the light of public policy and the law banning strikes in most of them. The table shows that for the economy as a whole, the proportion of trade disputes which resulted in strikes is rising - 49.8 per cent in 1975-76, 50.2 per cent in 1976-77 and 54.2 per cent in 1977-78.

The recorded causes of strikes in public enterprises are the usual ones relating to level of wages, hours of work, irregular or late payment of wages, bad physical conditions of work, etc. In the last couple of years, however, the main causes have stemmed from dissatisfaction with levels of salary gradings applied to the workers concerned, following upon the Udoji Public Service Salaries Review Commission Report, 1974. Teachers for their part have continuously been agitating, not only for upgrading but for better promotion prospects and implementation of fringe benefits to which they have become entitled since the Udoji Commission. Indeed, the tardiness in implementing agreed decisions has become one of the most potent sources of disputes and strikes in public enterprises.

There are no special legal provisions for dealing with disputes in public enterprises. They are accordingly dealt with in accordance with the procedures for mediation, conciliation and arbitration which we have outlined. The only exception of detail is that in respect of essential services the Commissioner for Labour can take the initiative in apprehending a dispute even if it has not been formally notified to him. But such disputes are still subject to resolution through the machinery outlined.

Personnel policies

By personnel policy we mean a set of well-defined principles which have been formulated to guide action with regard to the location, recruitment, development and effective utilisation of the human resources of an enterprise. So stated, only a minority of the public enterprises in Nigeria can be said to have established and operated effective personnel policies. The earlier corporations, such as the railways, coal, the Nigeria Electric Power Authority (NEPA), and ports, did in fact establish excellent personnel departments and formulated, under the influence of the colonial tradition, and the pressures of very active trade unions, personnel policies and practices which were printed and made available to the workers. Within such policies it was usual to recruit ordinary labour through heads of departments, but clerical, skilled labour, and high-level manpower were generally recruited through competitive tests and/or interview. Because of a shortage of skilled manpower in the country the enterprises established their own training institutions, the railway training school being for many years deservedly the most famous. Invariably, the handbooks declared promotion and advancement to be by merit. Under the pressures of the very powerful trade unions which existed in these enterprises, however, seniority tended to weigh much more heavily in promotion exercises.

Unfortunately, with the coming into power of political parties as independence approached, and since then, personnel principles in the old corporations were severely raped and, in the regions and later the states, the new boards and corporations made little or no effort at establishing personnel policies on scientific principles. The "spoils system" became rampant.

Membership of the boards of public enterprises came to be based largely on political considerations, and this extended to the senior permanent appointments as well. Soon, appointments to the lower positions became highly nepotic and, at all levels, ethnic and/or state considerations became also rampant. State-owned public enterprises are almost invariably fully staffed by indigenes of the State and, like the civil services, the principle of ethnic balance is very potent.

There is very little left in the public enterprise system to motivate workers. In the past, security of tenure, relatively high or competitive wages, generous holidays, and good retirement schemes constituted the main elements of worker motivation. Most of these have been cut down and no longer compare favourably with conditions in the private sector. The result, as we have noticed, is a high rate of labour turnover, inefficiency and inertia, in the public enterprises.

Workers' participation in decision making

The rationale for workers' participation in the decision making of the enterprise is that it is democratic, promotes worker commitment, improves labour-management relations, etc. So stated, the issue is deceptively simple, but in developing countries there are strong arguments against as well as for, workers' participation. However, "in Nigeria, the claim by workers to participation in management has as yet neither been loud nor sustained nor articulated".[1] For that very reason, and perhaps for ideological reasons, it is very little practised. Indeed, legal provision for worker participation in decision making in Nigeria has existed only in respect of some public enterprises - namely, the Nigerian Railway Corporation, the Nigerian Coal Corporation, the Nigerian Ports Authority, and the Electricity Corporation of Nigeria (ECN, now superseded by NEPA). The laws incorporating the Railways, the Ports Authority and the Electricity Corporation contained identical provisions to the effect that, of the members of the Board:

One person shall be a person appearing to the Minister, after considering any representations made by labour organisations

---

[1] T.M. Yesufu: The Dynamics of Industrial Relations, op. cit., Chapter VI.

concerned, to have had experience of, and to have shown capacity in, the organisation of workers.[1]

The governing law of the Nigerian Coal Corporation provided that:

> One member (i.e. of the Board) shall be appointed from among persons appearing to the Minister to be qualified as having had experience of industrial relations.[2]

As a result of these provisions a workers' representative was appointed to the Board of each of the enterprises concerned. Worker representation on boards of public enterprises has in fact been limited to these few parastatals, all of which, as the writer pointed out elsewhere, "were constituted in the 1950s and, like other practices of the colonial era, aped the British system of the times".[3] The multifarious public enterprises established since then have not incorporated the principle of workers' representation on boards or in decision making as such, and no government in the country since independence appears to have made any policy statement in that regard. Instead, the opinions and influence of workers on management decisions have been brought to bear through participation in joint consultative committees or collective bargaining.

III. Problems, trends and suggestions

Nigeria is at present undergoing serious and fundamental political and economic transition. So far as public enterprises are concerned, the only certainty is that they are here to stay, and any future government (federal or state) would have to face up to the problems - and they are serious - which beset the parastatals. Some of the questions which need to be answered may be summarised as follows:

- given the rationale for government establishment of public enterprises, are some of these enterprises in fact necessary?

- what should be the relationship between the public enterprises and their proprietor governments?

- how should the efficiency of public enterprises be improved?

- how should labour-management relations be improved?

These are random and general questions, and are far from exhaustive. The views that follow are also largely general and tentative. They nevertheless touch upon the most fundamental issues of parastatals at the present time.

We have seen that in developing countries there is no limit in principle to the extent that the State may intervene in the economic and social system to promote national development.

---

[1] See, for example, the Nigerian Railway Corporation Act, 1955, section 5(b)(iv).

[2] The Nigerian Coal Corporation Act, 1950, section 3(3).

[3] T.M. Yesufu: The Dynamics of Industrial Relations, op. cit.

Yet there are certain enterprises now undertaken under public entrepreneurship which can hardly be justified in an economy that still relies heavily on private enterprise, and in which there are so many alternative opportunities for government to invest its limited resources more productively. The involvement of a number of Nigerian States in road transportation is a case in point. Undertaking of municipal and intra-state transportation to promote movement between the rural areas and the cities as part of planned development is understandable. But the type of long-distance inter-state luxury coach transportation in which a number of States now indulge is highly unnecessary. In this field they are in competition with well organised private enterprises and individuals whose businesses are profitable, while those of the States are almost invariably making losses. Apart from tying down resources in unproductive enterprises, the losses are generally advanced as an argument for not raising the levels of wages of the workers concerned, to those prevailing in respect of their more profitable counterparts in the private sector. Perhaps even more significantly the incursion of governments into such fields as supermarkets, laundry and dry-cleaning services has been largely a failure. Even where they have succeeded, their contribution to the development of the sectors concerned, taking the state or country as a whole, has been little more than marginal. Some public enterprises which were established as pioneers, and for demonstration effect to hitherto reluctant private investors, such as textiles, have served their purpose. Again, almost invariably, their returns to investment tend to be lower than those of their private competitors.

It is important that governments should not rush into establishing enterprises at what appears at times to be no more than mere whims of influential individuals and those in authority. Proper feasibility studies should first be undertaken. Even then public enterprises should not be started merely because they are likely to be profitable. Governments should normally undertake only activities where no private investment is forthcoming. As soon as the sector is adequately covered by private enterprise the governments should withdraw and sell their interests to the public. Accordingly, regular reappraisals, preferably at development plan intervals, should be undertaken to review government commitments with a view to withdrawing from enterprises which are otherwise well covered, bearing in mind the need of the economy.

The issue of the relationship between public enterprises and their parent government is a fundamental one which received the serious attention of the Working Party on Statutory Corporations and Government-owned Companies to which we have already referred. The Federal Military Government accepted most of the recommendations of the Working Party to the effect, among other things, that:

- the Government will not interfere in the day-to-day administration of the corporations;

- ministerial control will be limited to purely policy matters, approval of by-laws, capital and operating budgets, and the fees and charges of the enterprises covered;

- cabinet control will also be confined only to certain well-defined areas, such as the appointment of chairmen and members of the boards of the enterprises, approving their loans, as well as the capital development and extension of their activities;

- that appointment to boards of public enterprises shall be
  depoliticised; accordingly, appointments will be made on the
  basis of the qualifications of individuals rather than their
  political views or party affiliation.[1]

There is no doubt that undue interference by governments in
the administration of the public enterprises has constituted one
of the greatest sources of their inefficiency. The politicisation
of the board membership was inevitably accompanied by nepotism in
staff appointments, which has had extremely deleterious effects
on worker morale and discipline, with predictable adverse effects
on labour-management relations in general. Under military rule
the tendency has been for government interference to increase, not
decrease. Even in matters of staff discipline, the governments
have on a number of occasions imposed measures such as retrenchment,
termination of appointments or dismissals, without the initiative
of, or prior reference to, the governing boards of the enterprises.
(With civilian rule pending, actions like these can only exacerbate
staff discontent and reduce their effectiveness of performance.)
It is therefore essential that the principles accepted in the policy
paper referred to above be re-enunciated and that the governments
should adhere to them strictly. Governments should desist from
taking panic measures every time a public enterprise makes a mistake
or earns public criticism. Private enterprises do make mistakes
and earn criticism. Long-term viability should be seen as more
important than the ability faceously to please at all times.
Public enterprises which operate within the competitive world of
private enterprise cannot be expected to succeed by being subjected
to inappropriate civil service codes and norms. Indeed, in
Nigerian conditions, open and competitive market pricing on the one
hand, and the rules and norms of civil service accountability on
the other, tend to be incompatible.

If the above suggestions are accepted and implemented, the
basic foundations of efficiency would have been laid. The imposition of the wages and conditions of service of the civil service
on the public enterprises should be abandoned. Workers and management should be left free to negotiate these terms within a well-defined national incomes policy, in the light of conditions prevailing in their respective industries. It is rather contradictory
for a government to use the big stick of its political power to
neutralise the employer responsibilities of public enterprise
management, in a country which even the Constitution declares to be
a mixed economy. In such conditions, if the Government establishes
a public enterprise to operate within the private sector, that
enterprise should be allowed to operate within the norms of private
enterprise - using the carrot and stick as appropriate to attain
viable levels of efficiency. The needs of efficiency demand that
management should have not only responsibility for an enterprise
but the power to effect that responsibility - to plan and take
decisions, including decisions relating to staff - the most
important but most volatile resource with which any enterprise
has to deal.

By reorganising and restructuring trade unions in Nigeria an
important step has been taken to improve labour-management relations
in public as well as in other enterprises. The unions are now more

---

[1] _The Policy of the Federal Military Government on Statutory Corporations and State-owned Companies_ (1968), op. cit.

articulate and stronger than they have ever been. But such power can be destructively used. It is essential that effective workers' and trade union education which forms a very important element in Nigeria's "new labour policy" be implemented without further delay. Such education should embrace the grass roots, the rank and file, as well as the top echelons of the unions. But management training is of equal importance in public enterprises. Very often, senior civil servants are deployed to assume important responsibilities in public enterprises for which they are most ill-prepared. The education and training required on both sides is one which should reorientate them fundamentally for mutual respect and accommodation. The machinery for conducting labour-management relations on a continuing basis - consultative committees, works councils, joint industrial councils, etc. - should be established at the appropriate levels and, above all, used regularly. It is vital that agreed decisions, particularly where they affect terms and conditions of employment, be implemented without undue delay - as we have seen, many of the trade disputes in public enterprises in recent years have been due to delays of this type.

IV. Conclusion

Public enterprises in Nigeria, as elsewhere, are an important instrument for social and economic development. They have proliferated in number and variety in the last 20 years. Many have not met the expectations of the founder governments or of the public at large. By reference to economic measures of efficiency most, indeed, can be said to have been failures. Some of them can be closed down without harm to anybody and others can be sold to private investors with benefit to all concerned. But the question is not how to do without public enterprises in general, but how they can be rationally restructured, organised, and their efficiency improved. In that task much more emphasis needs to be placed on the effective deployment and utilisation of the most important resource of the enterprises - the human resources. This requires, among other things, that the enterprises should become much more conscious of the need to improve labour-management relations as a means of promoting worker commitment, reducing labour turnover, and improving efficiency. If this can be done within reviewed public policies which liberalise government stranglehold on the enterprises, remove or minimise the deleterious effect of undue political interference, and give more emphasis to staff including managerial merit, an important step will have been taken in retrieving the image of public enterprises. All their problems would not have been solved. In the dynamic political, social and economic conditions in which they operate, final solutions are not possible. But it is important that their situations, underlying rationale, and methods be regularly appraised.

ANNEX

TRADE DISPUTES IN NIGERIA BY EMPLOYMENT SECTORS, 1975-78

Year	Employment sector	Total No. of disputes recorded	Disputes resulting in strikes		Workers involved		Man-days lost	
			No.	% of total	No.	% of total	No.	% of total
1	2	3	4	5	6	7	8	9
1975-76	Private sector	443	225	84.0	80 692	51.5	305 992	61.3
	Civil service	45	20(18)	7.5	59 087	37.7	111 402	22.3
	Education sector	23	13(5)	4.8	12 230	7.8	46 276	9.3
	Parastatals	27	10(9)	3.7	4 542	2.9	35 133	7.0
	Total	538	268	100	156 551	100	498 803	100
				49.8				
1976-77	Private sector	262	132	89.8	75 122	84.5	234 244	88.1
	Civil service	18	7(6)	4.8	7 263	8.2	14 296	5.4
	Education sector	3	3	2.0	1 900	2.1	4 124	1.6
	Parastatals	10	5	3.4	4 622	5.2	13 070	4.9
	Total	293	147	100	88 957	100	265 734	100
				50.2				
1977-78	Private sector	209	121	80.7	60 418	53.7	203 234	38.4
	Civil service	41	14(12)	9.3	8 517	7.6	63 276	11.9
	Education sector	12	6(5)	4.0	36 159	32.2	242 751	45.9
	Parastatals	15	9(8)	6.0	7 325	6.5	20 182	3.8
	Total	277	150	100	112 419	100	529 443	100
				54.2				

Source: Ministry of Labour Records.

The figures in brackets in column 4 indicate the number of disputes for which strikes statistics were available.

LABOUR-MANAGEMENT RELATIONS IN
TUNISIAN PUBLIC ENTERPRISES

by

N. Ladhari,

Directorate of Social Security,
Ministry of Social Affairs,
Tunisia

PART I - GENERAL

Chapter 1 - Grounds for the setting up of public enterprises

The importance of the economic sector managed more or less directly by the public authorities depends on the evolution of governmental concepts of state prerogatives and responsibilities with respect to economic activities. These activities sometimes produce quite considerable profits and have far-reaching repercussions on the national income in general and the level of individual incomes. They directly affect prices and wages, the level of employment, industrial peace and, in the long run, the stability of a country's economic and social policy, in view of the fact that the conditions governing a country's production determine the pattern of its society. Therefore the State cannot fail to concern itself with the nation's economic life.

1. The ideas underlying the evolution of the State's role

For a long time, during the era of economic liberalism, the State could confine itself to purely administrative tasks such as maintaining order and ensuring defence, leaving profit-making activities to the individual, since, according to theory, the interests of the various parties should eventually coincide with the general interest. An evolution in economic concepts and social relations, which had started in the nineteenth century, gained strength in the twentieth due to the growth of new ideas regarding equality, democracy and trade unionism and the enormous expansion in State responsibilities resulting from the two world wars and economic crises. This evolution induced governments not to leave the leading role in economic production to the private individual.

This led to interventionism marked by State participation in undertakings, State control, the direct management of certain activities by the public authorities, or even the introduction of State monopoly in certain sectors or throughout the national economy, the nation as a whole then becoming the sole owner of all means of production. This evolution, varying in scale from one country to another, is naturally governed by a wide range of domestic factors such as the political and social awakening of the masses, their cultural level, the particular mentality of each nation, the religion, and educational level, the influence of trade unions and tradition, the availability of local capital and the dynamism of the ruling classes. Consideration also has to be given to the external environment and the influence of factors which condition economic life at the international level.

2. The relevant situation in Tunisia

    (a) Prior to independence

Prior to the achievement of independence, economic life in Tunisia was guided by principles established by the protecting power, in this case, France. These were based on liberalism,

which itself stemmed from the old colonial agreement. The dependent
country had to supply raw materials and purchase the manufactured
goods.   Maintenance of the native population in poor living conditions constituted the best guarantee for its submissivity. The
economy was essentially a primary one, devoted to widespread agriculture and mining. The mines were managed as concessions granted
to French companies and the sole State income from these activities
was in the form of taxes. In addition to the mines, there were
public services, which were also run as concessions in accordance
to a list of specifications given by public authorities. This was
the case in the railways - the Tunisian Railway Company, CFT
(Compagnie fermière des chemins de fer tunisiens), the Phosphates
and Sfax-Gafsa Railway Company (Compagnie des phosphates et des
chemins de fer de Sfax-Gafsa), urban rail or tram transportation
for Tunis and its suburbs or by road - the Tunisian Road Transport
Company, TAT (Société tunisienne automobile des transports) and the
Tunisian Road Transport Company for the Sahel, STTAS (Société
tunisienne des transports automobiles du Sahel), and electricity,
gas and water supplies.

As a result of the change in economic and social conditions
between the two world wars and under pressure from the workers and
unions, the State stepped in to regulate employment within the
companies holding public service concessions. This action was the
subject of a decree of 19 May 1938, adopted by the French Popular
Front, whose time in office was marked, in both Tunisia and France,
by far-reaching social reforms such as paid leave, collective agreements and the 40-hour week. Moreover, the new statutes introduced
by this decree were generally applied to the personnel of the
public service concessions and the State permanent workers and
employees and those of the local governments and public establishments. Thus, already at that time, it appeared that the labour
force of the undertakings running the public services - even though
these were not operating under state-control - was to be assimilated
to that of the public administrations. This feature was maintained
and even reinforced subsequently.

The concessions system was still embodied in the liberal economy
whose weaknesses had been revealed by the economic crisis preceding
the Second World War. Consequently, the State found itself forced
to intervene in order to protect the general interests and to save
undertakings in difficulty, especially those with a large labour
force and providing a public service. This intervention took the
form of a decree adopted on 30 January 1937, which organised State
control over firms, associations and organisations of all types
requiring its assistance or that of the regional or local administrations and public establishments. In exchange for this assistance,
the State was justified in extending its control over the operation
of the undertakings.

During and after the Second World War, State control was made
necessary by the requirements of the war and the prevailing shortages.
The evolution of ideas amongst the ruling classes and pressure groups
with respect to the State's role in economic life was determined by
wartime difficulties.

State control over the economy was thus reinforced in Tunisia,
as in France. The State was obliged to concern itself with the
situation in the mining undertakings with a large workforce, which
were in difficulty, in order to safeguard employment. This was
the purpose of a decree of 17 October 1941, a text subsequently

replaced by the decree of 1 April 1948, which was wider in scope as it related to all firms and groups in which the State had capital interests. This decree stipulates that the State was to be represented on the boards of management of these bodies on a scale proportionate to its holdings, provided that it had not less than two seats and not more than two-thirds of the total number. Furthermore, it appoints a technical controller and an auditor for them.

(b) After independence

Following Tunisia's attainment of independence and in conformity with the protocol of 20 March 1956, the new Government had to orient the nation's economy in different directions.

The mass departure of foreign capitalists, the weakness of local capital, the rarity or even non-existence of major industrial leaders, the population's poor living conditions - which restricts its ability to save and invest - its very low levels of vocational and technical training, a widespread spirit of equality throughout the population resulting in hostility to the artificial creation of a society in which riches could be concentrated in the hands of a minority as a result of the forces of the capitalist economy, the fact also that many means of production previously controlled by the protecting power or its nationals were to be returned to the State of Tunisia, all these were factors which contributed to the State becoming the main driving force of the economy, as it was considered to be the surest upholder of the general interests. Furthermore, the State had to step in in order to compensate for the weaknesses of certain heads of undertakings or their unwillingness to collaborate.

Many of the latter, especially the foreigners, left the country, taking their capital with them, thus disrupting economic life and aggravating the social problems. Consequently, the State had to set up new deposit and trade banks and take over the management of a multitude of undertakings which were in danger of breaking up as a result of these departures. It was also obliged to bring under State control the undertakings holding concessions for the provision of public services, which were disorganised for the same reasons. Moreover, maintenance of the concessions system would not have been compatible with the Government's policies with regard to the economy and income distribution. The new leaders, who had emerged from the masses, were convinced that direct management was in better agreement with the interest of the nation and they did away with the unnecessary dividends which had previously been paid out by the private capitalists.

Economic activities were therefore to be managed primarily by the State, which had decided to draw up plans covering all fields, in which creative initiatives by the public authorities were to play the major role. Many undertakings were reorganised and others were created from nothing to satisfy the urgent requirements of an economy obliged to develop in order to cover the needs of a society which had recovered its responsibility for progress towards greater well-being.

The predominant role of the State was strengthened by the legislative decree of 3 April 1962, which provided that the creation, extension, conversion, or displacement of any industrial undertaking required prior approval by the public authorities. This clear orientation towards State control and capitalism, established from the time planning started, was to evolve in accordance with the decisions taken by the successive congresses of the party in power.

3. Move towards socialisation

The "Congress of Destiny" of October 1964 drew up plans for an integrated socialist approach. On this occasion, the party previously referred to as "Destourian", i.e. constitutional, assumed the designation of "Socialist" and adopted the following principles:

> Ownership is a social function the exercise of which is subordinate to the general interests; it must serve to achieve the national objectives. This is the fundamental condition for it to be exercised, to be respected by the society and protected by the State.

The following guidelines were approved:

- modern industries corresponding to the country's present and future potential are to be created and extended;

- economic and social development is to be achieved in accordance with a scientific plan;

- the State is to maintain supreme control over all economic sectors; it has to intervene in the event of inefficiency on the part of individuals, situations prejudicial to the general interests or bad management;

- in the case of agriculture; socialism is to lead to collectivisation;

- as regards industry, the State is to manage the basic activities in order to ensure economic progress, and those undertakings which are conducive to the development of secondary activities; economic expansion must not be subordinate to the sole criterion of profit;

- industrial development is to be promoted in the underdeveloped regions; the private sector, aware of socialist aims, is to be entrusted with the task of establishing undertakings in the non-essential fields;

- the public and private sectors are to be co-ordinated along socialist lines;

- workers have to participate in fulfilment of the responsibilities and obligations of their undertakings;

- as regards trade, the State must create national bodies for the importation and distribution of goods.

Application of these principles should lead to the generalisation of agricultural and trading co-operatives and the expansion of industrial public enterprises.

4. Temporary halt of socialism and
   partial return to private management

In 1969 it was found that socialisation of the economy had been a failure. Large state-run industrial undertakings had deficits and collectivisation of the land had resulted in lower production. This realisation led to the revision of the Government's approach to the economic situation during the "Congress of Clarification" in October 1971.

The new orientations were as follows: as regards agriculture, the State would have the right to sell state-owned lands to private persons. In the case of industry, the establishment of industries must be governed by the country's potential, the financial and human resources available and market conditions. Preference must be given to small- and medium-scale enterprises, without excluding certain industrial sectors, particularly those involved in the transformation of mining products, with due consideration for the potential market demand. The State must also encourage the private and co-operative sectors.

This meant that the State was no longer playing the exclusive, or even the leading role in the economy. Its activities were to be restricted to those public enterprises providing services and in areas where it was necessary to fill the gap in private initiative.

The part to be played by the State in the economy was confirmed during the "Congress of Clarity" which took place in September 1974 and stressed that the creation of national undertakings had to be realistic and should correspond to good management. The major industries must revolve round the processing of mining products, such as phosphates, oil and iron. The State had to promote the industries supplying consumer goods, especially the food industry, and to develop the processing industries; such as textiles, leather and clothing. Industrialisation had to be conceived to create the largest possible number of jobs and ensure a balanced development of the regions and encouragement was to be given to foreign investment for the establishment of exporting industries likely to increase employment opportunities.

In the agricultural sector, State lands would continue to be sold to private persons while the State would merely keep the model farms.

It can be seen from these decisions that the new approach was to give the private sector a leading role in the control of the economy, while the State was to continue to manage the public services, serve as a model employer and act as a driving force for the promotion of the private sector. All public and private economical activities should be in conformity with the plan established by the State.

Chapter 2 - Definition of public enterprises

1. **Legislation**

Act 68-13 of 3 June 1968 defined a general statute for the workforce of public enterprises which included all undertakings and bodies of all types engaged in economic activities, that is to say, producing or exchanging goods or services, in which the State or local public bodies and public establishments directly or indirectly hold shares. The State was not obliged to hold a minimum percentage of capital, whereas other public bodies and undertakings must hold at least 10 per cent.

A public enterprise may take the form of a limited liability company, a national company, an office or a public industrial or commercial establishment. This definition thus excludes public administrations and establishments of an administrative nature, which have no economic objective or investment capital, with only fixed assets and an annual budget. At the same time, it is Tunisian practice to include amongst public enterprises those State monopolies, such as the national printing office (Imprimerie officielle), which pursue a given economic activity. In practice, employees of these monopolies are governed by the same rules as the civil servants and State workers. This applies even when the monopoly has been declared a public industrial or commercial establishment, as for instance the state tobacco and matches monopoly. The labour-management relations of the monopolies do not fall within the scope of this study.

On the other hand, this practice has resulted in the inclusion amongst public enterprises of those bodies which are not truly economic units, but are administrative or public services having only very incidental, if any, economic activities, to which it was desired to leave greater managerial freedom by giving them an industrial and commercial character. This enabled them to escape from the prior financial controls on expenditure which administrative services usually have to endure. This applies, for instance, to the National Social Security Fund (Caisse nationale de sécurité sociale), the National Pensions and Social Welfare Fund (Caisse nationale de retraite et de prévoyance sociale), the Office for Expatriate Tunisian Workers, Employment and Vocational Training (Office des travailleurs tunisiens à l'étranger, de l'emploi et de la formation professionnelle), etc.

These bodies are in fact detached branches of the administration, possessing a certain autonomy due to decentralisation of the individual services. They possess no capital properly speaking although they often receive appropriations, and production or trade do not constitute their essential objectives, although some of them may undertake such activities incidentally. Moreover, the funds of these bodies may not be public, but come solely from private persons, as is the case for instance, with the National Social Security Fund. This is financed solely by employers' and workers' contributions, without any State support. The latter, which has supervisory rights, is merely responsible for safeguarding the general interest. However, as these bodies have been given an industrial or commercial, or even financial, character, they have passed into the ranks of public enterprises.

Thus, public enterprises encompass all bodies of a commercial nature, whether in form or substance. Their capital generally makes them totally or partially responsible to the State or a legal entity under public law (State, government, local authority, public establishment). Public enterprises usually receive a capital endowment as well as moveables and real estate. Nevertheless, some assimilated bodies, considered as public enterprises, may possess funds which are not truly speaking public, but which concern the public interest.

2. Dividing line between the private and public sectors

Ownership of the capital constitutes the primary criterion for distinguishing between the public and private sectors. When the State or a subordinate legal entity under public law (government, local authority, public establishment) holds part of the capital, it is a public enterprise. This constitutes grounds for State supervision with all which that implies as regards power of management and control. Other bodies considered secondarily as public enterprises are those responsible for the decentralised management of public services in accordance with general law. They may also be public utility bodies created by private groups. None of the latter bodies possess capital in the true sense. Their funds are generally provided by the public authorities and sometimes by private persons.

3. Composition of the public sector

Even now, after the cessation of socialisation, the public sector includes a very large number of undertakings in all fields of activity to the extent that it employs a very large, if not the major, proportion of the entire national labour force.

New undertakings are established from time to time whenever it is felt necessary to launch an activity in one or another sector, as it is a fact that the State still constitutes the main driving force for national development in all fields.

In practice, all these undertakings, with the exception of State monopolies, are subject to the same regulations in their relations with the State. On legal grounds, some of them have been declared public industrial or commercial establishments. This group includes all those which manage public services, particularly certain national companies (e.g. the Tunisian National Railways Company - SNCFT,[1] the National Transport Company - SNT,[2] the Tunisian Electricity and Gas Company - STEG,[3] the National Company for the Exploitation and Distribution of Water - SONEDE)[4] and all the offices. (Other bodies have simply been declared to be of public interest (e.g. the trade groups for vegetables, dates and fruit).) All other public enterprises have the status of

---

[1] Société nationale des chemins de fer tunisiens.

[2] Société nationale des transports.

[3] Société tunisienne d'electricité et du gaz.

[4] Société nationale d'exploitation et de distribution des eaux.

commercial companies. This distinction is important because public establishments as a whole enjoy certain privileges, particularly those which they obtained under an old decree of 15 February 1904 providing exemptions from certain liabilities. They also enjoy financial advantages, such as tax exemptions and preferential treatment for their credits. Some public establishments have even been granted public authority prerogatives: the power, like that of the fiscal administrations, to issue "liquidation orders" against their debtors, i.e. compulsory sales orders against the property of their debtors, without the need for prior judiciary procedures.

Chapter 3 - Historical evolution and present importance of public enterprises

Public enterprises have one of two origins: some were taken over by the State and some were created as entirely new bodies in application of the Government's economic policies. These two categories exist for both the undertakings managing public services and those which are economic units.

During an initial phase, the State decided to intervene in the operation of certain undertakings, especially when they were managing a public service or when the size of their labour force and the role played by them in the national economy was such that the public authorities could not deviate from their responsibility as regards their future operations.

The personnel of these companies holding public service concessions served the public interests in the same way as the public service employees. It therefore was normal that the public authorities should supervise their activities more closely. Consequently, the statute of their personnel was detached from general legislation. It has been mentioned that in 1938, whilst these undertakings were still part of the concessions system, their personnel was granted a statute distinct from that of general labour legislation, but very similar to that of the public service. This same personnel had been granted a retirement pensions scheme under a Decree of 28 August 1948, very similar to that of public service personnel, which had been set up at the beginning of the protectorate in 1898. As regards social security, it was covered by a social security scheme instituted by a Decree of 13 December 1951, similar to that of the public servants promulgated by the Decree of 12 April 1951, whilst workers in the private sector had to wait for Act 60-30 of 14 December 1960 to obtain social security coverage and the Decree of 27 April 1974 to be entitled to retirement pensions.

After independence, as a result of the exodus of capital and foreign technicians and also due to the Government's priorities, the State took over responsibility for management of the transport concession companies (railways, urban and suburban transport, road transport), and electricity, gas and water supplies and replaced them by new national companies (SNCFT, SNT, STEG, SONEDE). It also bought back the stock held by foreign companies. This was, for instance, the case with Air France from which certain capital was taken to establish Tunis Air.

Moreover, and in the same connection, the State created new national companies in order to satisfy the needs of an independent country by providing the management needed for public services in various fields. In particular, it set up a National Navigation Company, a Lighterage and Handling Company, a National Ports Office, an Airports Office, a Trade Office, a National Real Estate Office and a Press Office.

In a second stage, the State had to intervene in certain economic sectors which were not public services, either in order to save them from their difficulties and thus safeguard employment, or to initiate and manage widely differing economic activities so as to develop national production and raise the people's living standards.

These two types of motivations were frequently combined as a result of policy decisions taken by the Government. For example, the State recovered full control of the mining undertakings (phosphates and iron), which were in difficulty. It also extended its action in the oil industry by creating several undertakings in that sector or by participating with foreign firms in the founding of similar undertakings.

In accordance with its international policy and socialistic ideology, the State launched many undertakings in all fields in order to protect the general interest from excessive private profit making and also to provide a model and a driving force for private initiative. It set up a wide range of companies in almost all sectors, such as: textiles, chemicals, iron and steel making, metallurgy, food industries, building, tourism, banking, insurance, agriculture and information.

Public enterprises are the most important bodies in all sectors of the economy as regards both the number of persons employed and their activities and accomplishments.

According to the latest statistics taken from the 1975 census, there is an economically active population of 1,621,820 in Tunisia from a total of 5,608,000 inhabitants. The number of paid workers is reported to be 872,070 while the total for State officials and workers is 129,351. During the same period, public industrial or commercial undertakings employed about 250,000 persons, representing about 28.66 per cent of all wage earners. State employees together with public law personnel including the staff of the administrations add up to 379,351, i.e. 43.5 per cent of all wage earners.

In reality, the statistics do not cover the personnel of all public enterprises. They relate particularly to public enterprises of an industrial and commercial nature, or those which run the public services, or those which are significantly large scaled. Many undertakings of various sizes but of an essentially economic nature and whose capital is either entirely or partially owned by the State or by legal entities under public law were counted as private undertakings. The workforce of the public enterprises certainly represents more than the 28.66 per cent and when the officials and workers of the administrations are taken into account the State may be the largest employer in the country.

PART II - LABOUR-MANAGEMENT RELATIONS IN PUBLIC ENTERPRISES

Chapter 1 - Legal framework

1. **Legislation applicable to public enterprises**

   From the point of view of labour legislation, public enterprises in Tunisia are subject to a system based to a large extent on that of the civil service, but maintaining links with the general labour legislation. Act 68-13 of 3 June 1968 granted the workers of public enterprises a general status which is a perfect counterpart of the civil servants' status adopted by an Act 68-12 of that same date. However, it is specified in section two of Act 68-13 that where there is no specific provision in this Act, they are subject to the general labour legislation (Labour Code and collective agreements). This assimilation to public service law is attributable to the fact that for a long time the latter was better developed and more precise than that governing workers in the private sector.

   Most State officials in Tunisia during the period of the French protectorate were French and from the beginning of the colonial regime they were granted a certain status prior to the enactment of labour legislation. In any case, the latter developed as successive adjunctions and the Labour Code which combined and systematised these elements was not promulgated until after independence, by an Act of 30 April 1966. Workers in the private or para-public sector have always considered the public service system as a model and their claims have been designed to acquire the same rights and safeguards as State employees, which were for a long time considered as privileged. Thus, the first statute for personnel of the undertakings running public service concessions, that of 19 May 1938, was also applicable to established State workers and was patterned on the public service statute of 7 February 1936.

   Taken as a whole, the labour policy relating to public enterprises takes its form from a general statute inspired by that of the civil service, especially as regards all items affecting the career of officials (general obligations, recruitment, personal reports and promotion, discipline, leave, termination of employment).

   The provisions of the general statute for public enterprises must be completed by specific statutes for each undertaking prescribing the organisation of work within the undertaking, stipulating the specific obligations and advantages, especially as regards leave, social rights and, in particular, establishing a wages scale.

   It is agreed that where no provision exists in the general statute, the general legislation represented by the Labour Code is applicable to the personnel of public enterprises. Nevertheless, if more favourable conditions peculiar to the occupational branch are established by special statutes or collective agreements, they take priority over the relevant legal provisions which mostly provide for minimum conditions. This applies particularly to rest periods and sick leave. Consequently, the situation of public enterprises is governed de juris and de facto by the general statute as completed by the specific statute of each undertaking. Reference is made to the Labour Code and collective agreements only as a complementary measure, as these relate in principle only to private undertakings.

It must be pointed out that pursuant to section 68 of Act 68-13 of 3 June 1968, the special statutes of public enterprises had to be promulgated by decree within one year from the entry into force of the general statute. Since then, some statutes have been drawn up and promulgaged by decree, sometimes simply by a letter from the Prime Minister. However, ten years later, there are still many undertakings for which no special statutes have been decreed, such undertakings continue to be governed by the general statute and by general labour legislation, collective agreements and the Labour Code.

2. Collective agreements and public enterprises

It was clear from the outset that the special statute is an alternative to a collective agreement. The special statute is a form of labour regulation in which participation by the public authorities is more apparent because the employer is in fact the State. Consequently, there is no negotiation between labour and management, as it the case for collective agreements, where the State ratifies the agreement reached, by means of an approval order. In this case, there are certainly close contacts between workers' representatives united within a union and the management of the public enterprises which, in principle, drafts the statute and submits it to the public authorities for approval. The draft statute first has to be approved by the responsible minister and is then submitted to the Prime Minister, who is responsible for controlling all special statutes in the same way as that of the public service. It is the Prime Minister who issues the decree ratifying the final statute.

The public authorities have complete latitude to determine the provisions of the statute before it is made mandatory by decree. Although the statute is officially the result of regulatory action and not of a collective agreement, it is nevertheless the outcome of informal consultations between the management and the union of the undertaking concerned, and can obtain the backing of the central union.

It should be noted that, generally speaking, the managing director is responsible for establishing the works rules and personnel policy. The works rules are referred to the management board which sometimes includes a representative of the workers or the central union. Furthermore, a record of all the management board's discussions is submitted to the responsible authority.

In addition to the technical supervision exercised by the responsible ministry, the approval of the Ministry of Finance is sought for all decisions having financial implications. A technical supervisor is frequently assigned to a public enterprise in order to control, on behalf of the responsible ministry, the technical aspects of all the undertaking's activities and its general administration. He attends all meetings of the board of management and may apply a suspensive veto, on behalf of the minister he represents, on any of the board's decisions. On the other hand, an auditor is always nominated by the Ministry of Finance for the public enterprises, to follow all measures having financial implications; he can veto any decision which he considers contrary to the interests of the undertaking or the State. In the event of the auditor raising an objection, it is the appropriate minister who takes the final decision.

The Decree of 1 April 1948 already provided for the nomination of a technical supervisor and an auditor in all companies in which the State or a local public authority holds shares. When it is an office or other public enterprise of an industrial or commercial nature, there is always an auditor. But sometimes the statutes do not provide for the nomination of a technical supervisor, either because his supervision on day-to-day management is not considered necessary, or simply for reasons of convenience.

Chapter 2 - The occupational organisations

1. Unionisation of the workers

Workers of public enterprises enjoy the same right of association as all wage earners of the private sector. Article 12 of the general statutes states: "In accordance with the legislation in force, trade union rights are recognised for the workers governed by these statutes."

There are no special provisions - either preferential or prejudicial - in this field regarding the workers of public enterprises. Public enterprises are at least as widely unionised as in the private sector.

Workers of all types and ranks in public enterprises are free to join the trade unions which are affiliated to the single central union of the country: the General Labour Union of Tunisia (UGTT) (Union générale tunisienne du travail). Consequently, this organisation embodies both the officials and workers of the national undertakings and those of private undertakings, whether agricultural or non-agricultural.

The prevailing form of organisation in Tunisia is the industrial union, combining all the workers of a given branch independently of their trade. Workers in public enterprises can form one or more union sections affiliated to a federation grouping all workers in the branch of activity in question.

Local unions may be organised on a territorial basis and group all the workers in a section of the undertaking within a given region. This is the case for instance of the Tunisian Railway Company (SNCFT), whose personnel is divided into regional sections: three in Tunis, one in Sfax, one in Sousse, one in Gafsa, one in Metlaoui, one in Gaafour and one in Meknassy. Unions may also be divided up according to the departmental breakdown of the undertaking, each with a specific function. The National Transport Company, for instance, has three unions: one for administrative personnel, one for the technical department and one for the operations department. Within each department; the entire workforce is represented, as in the industrial union, from the engineers down to the labourers.

The federations themselves are affiliated with the central union as full members. It must be pointed out also that the various unions of the UGTT in each activity are also grouped on a regional basis within regional unions which are subordinated to the central union.

No union security arrangements, such as the closed shop practised in some countries, are established by law or agreement. However, the workers may themselves feel that it is useful to join a union in order to act as a group in defending their interests. The number of union members is relatively large; they represent between 40 and 80 per cent of all workers. In addition, unionised workers have better chances of putting forward their views because, in practice, only unionised workers are represented, by either their local union or the UGTT, during discussions with the employer or the State in the many commissions responsible for the settlement of workers' problems. The UGTT alone is authorised to negotiate collective agreements or to discuss wage increases and reviews. Since the enactment of Law 77-55 of 3 August 1977, it is also the UGTT which is competent to nominate candidates to serve as members of the conciliation boards. This law replaces elections by nominations made by orders issued by the Ministry of Social Affairs acting upon proposals from the most representative trade unions and employers' organisations. Choice is simplified by the fact that only single central unions exist. The UGTT has also claimed the sole right to put forward candidates for works committees.

In practice, on account of the number of such undertakings, their organisation and cohesion, the representatives of workers of public enterprises play a leading role within unions in the handling of matters concerning all the workers in the public and private sectors. It is they who show the greatest dynamism in relations with the employers. Action taken by the union representatives of the Public enterprises, either public service such as the railways and road transportation, or purely economic undertakings such as the mines, has the greatest impact on the country's social life and has a tendency to draw the attention of union representatives of the private undertakings. This applies in particular to strikes and claims concerning wages and related advantages.

2. Organisation of employers

In Tunisia, the employers, like the workers, are free to form associations of their own choosing. Indeed, the heads of non-agricultural undertakings are associated in a central union, the Tunisian Union of Industry, Trade and Crafts (UTICA) (Union tunisienne de l'industrie, du commerce et de l'artisanat), whereas farmers have formed the National Farmers' Union (UNA) (Union nationale des agriculteurs). The leaders of the employers' associations participate as social partners, beside the representatives of the State and the workers' unions, in drawing up and applying social policy throughout the country with respect to collective agreements, wages policy, collective disputes, etc.

Many heads of public enterprises, especially those involved in ordinary economic activities not constituting a public service, are affiliated with UTICA as full members and some of them play a leading role in the administration of the various federations as well as in the supervisory bodies of the Central Employers' Association itself. The representatives of the national undertakings are thus able to participate in the conclusion of collective agreements applicable to the sectors to which they belong when no specific statute has been promulgated by decree as foreseen in Act 68-13 of 3 June 1968.

As only a few public enterprises have been given a specific statute, all the others, in particular those managing a purely economic activity, without being a monopoly, comply with general labour legislation, including to a large extent the collective agreements of the branch to which they belong. This applies to, amongst others, the metallurgical, building, paper, wood, building materials, banking and insurance branches.

Moreover, the heads of national undertakings concerned are actively involved in the conclusion of collective agreements relating to their respective sector. This was the case for example when collective agreements were being negotiated for banking, insurance, the milk industries, ports and docks, mechanical industries, building, and retail trade.

However, heads of the major national undertakings having the status of public industrial or commercial establishments, like the offices and national companies managing public services, appointed directly or indirectly by the State, subject to its control and applying directives emanating from the public authorities, have no interest in joining employers' organisations. This stems from the fact that they are State agents, entrusted with management on behalf of the State, whereas private employers have private interests to defend. Moreover, the latter are obliged in practice to comply with directives of the State which, as guardian of public order, acts as referee in the event of conflict of interests, and maintains a balance between the various elements of the society. This explains the unquestionable State leadership in the management of all sectors of economic and social life.

3. Recognition of the unions

Although nothing in Tunisian legislation prohibits the setting up of several unions in one enterprise, in practice there exist only one single employers' organisation and one single central union: the UGTT for the workers, UTICA for employers in the non-agricultural sector and UNA for agricultural undertakings. This simplifies recognition of the unions. It is therefore unnecessary to determine the most representative unions to have the exclusive right to negotiate with the employers and the State.

Chapter 3 - Labour-management relations

1. Collective bargaining

As stated already, public enterprises are governed in principle by a general statute complemented by special statutes. It is these statutes which determine the careers of workers and fix working and wage conditions. The latter are established in detail following a scale, as in the public service. General legislation as represented by the Labour Code and collective agreements is applicable to them on a secondary basis. The collective agreement of 23 March 1973 establishes the general regulations applicable throughout the non-agricultural sector. In addition, specific collective agreements for certain activities can be applied to workers in the national undertakings to the extent that their statutes have made no stipulations regarding certain points or when their provisions are less favourable, particularly as regards leave.

In reality, some undertakings, particularly those pursuing ordinary economic activities, that is to say, not providing public services, are governed by collective agreements in the same way as private establishments exercising similar activities. Many collective agreements have been concluded either for the national undertakings alone or for national and private undertakings simultaneously, such as for instance the collective agreement for banks, which applies to all public or private banks with the exception of the Central Bank; the collective agreement for the milk industry, applicable in particular to the Tunisian Milk Industries Company (STIL) (Société tunisienne des industries laitières) and to Tunisie-Lait, which are public enterprises; the collective agreement for the building materials industries, which covers national undertakings in particular, the collective agreement for insurance companies, etc.

The collective agreements concluded in Tunisia are of a general nature; they are valid for an entire sector of activity and cover the entire country. The legislation provides the possibility of special agreements for specific establishments. These are concluded either within a general agreement or autonomously, but in the latter case they call for a special authorisation by an order from the Minister of Social Affairs. About ten agreements of the latter type have been concluded. Collective agreements are negotiated at central level, i.e. in the Ministry of Social Affairs, under the aegis of the State, between representatives of the two central organisations, that of the workers and that of the employers. The ministers responsible for the public enterprises are represented during negotiations when a public enterprise is concerned. After a general agreement has been concluded between the parties, it does not become applicable until it has been approved by an order from the Minister of Social Affairs.

All collective agreements follow the same pattern: definition of scope, period of validity, trade union rights and workers' representation, career organisation, working conditions, remuneration, leave, discipline, organisation of a joint consultative commission, vocational training, social rights, and special advantages.

The agreements also contain definitions of the various categories of personnel and are always complemented by a detailed wages scale.

Once a collective agreement has been approved, it becomes binding on all employers and workers falling within its scope of application. Workers of the national undertakings concerned are governed by this agreement to the extent that they are not covered by a more favourable specific statute adopted in application of Act 68-13 of 3 June 1968.

The provisions of these collective agreements apply to all categories of the undertaking's personnel, from top to bottom, with the exception of the managing director selected from amongst civil servants and who usually continues to belong to the civil service, at least as regards advancement in seniority and pension entitlements. However, although he may continue to receive his former remuneration as a civil servant, the managing director of a public enterprise prefers to receive the salary fixed in the undertaking because its salary scale is generally more favourable (for all categories of worker) than that of the civil service.

The personnel of a public enterprise may also comprise, especially amongst the supervisory grades, officials detached from the civil service. These are nevertheless governed by the regulations applicable to all the personnel of the undertaking - special statute or collective agreement - as regards career organisation, discipline, remuneration, social advantages, etc. They generally retain the advantages offered by the civil service, especially as regards promotion, seniority rights and retirement entitlements.

The example set by collective agreements of major national undertakings such as the bank, may have a stimulating effect, on similar undertakings and even on private undertakings. This is especially so with regard to benefits obtained, such as paid leave longer than that foreseen by law, various supplements to wages amounting even to a fifteenth month's wage, wider social security entitlements in respect of sickness, maternity, death, social assistance, accommodation, etc.

2. Labour disputes

Generally speaking, the workers of public enterprises are subject, as regards labour disputes, to the general legislation established by the Labour Code. Consequently, individual disputes can be referred to the labour inspectorate for a possible solution at an administrative level, and eventually to the labour courts for a judicial solution. It must be noted, however, that forcible execution is not possible against public enterprises which are classified as public institutions.

In the case of collective disputes, the Labour Code (Chapter XIII, Vol. VII, the provisions of which were recast by Act 73-77 of 8 December 1973 and Act 76-84 of 11 August 1976) applies equally to both private and public enterprises. If there is a threat to the national interest, compulsory arbitration can take place in respect of either a public or a private undertaking.

The procedure applicable for the settlement of a collective dispute, strike, or lockout consists of several phases each offering the possibility of a solution. These are:

(1) reference to the undertaking's joint structures: joint administrative commission, and works committee;

(2) reference to the regional conciliation bureau or, if this does not exist, to the regional labour inspectorate and then to the regional or the central arbitration board. A ten-day period of notice has to be given prior to a strike or a lockout.

The regional board under the chairmanship of the regional governor and comprising equal representation of the workers and employers, is competent when the conflict involves a local undertaking. The central board, which is chaired by the Minister of

Social Affairs and comprises an equal number of workers' and employers' representatives, acts when the conflict covers several administrative regions or the entire national territory.

A strike or a lockout occurring after failure of arbitration procedures has to be approved by the central union or employers' association concerned.

(3) Voluntary and joint submission to arbitration. In this case, the arbitrator is designated by the two parties or, in the event of failure to agree, by the Minister of Social Affairs.

(4) Reference of the dispute to compulsory arbitration when there is a risk of the strike or lockout being prejudicial to the national interest. The single arbitrator is then designated by the Prime Minister.

The decision of the arbitrator; whether selected by the parties or imposed by the Ministry, is binding and final. The Act of 11 August 1976 provided that a list of arbitrators would be established by order of the Minister of Social Affairs after consultation with the central employers' and workers' organisations (this list has not yet been published).

Strikes or lockouts which may take place without recourse to these compulsory arbitration procedures or in violation of the arbitrator's decision, or without the approval of the central association concerned are illegal. Those responsible and persons who participated are liable to penal sanctions including imprisonment or fines. The same sanctions are applicable for the occupation of work premises during an illegal strike, and the sabotage of equipment or its improper use.

Requisition of the undertaking or its personnel may be decided by decree when a strike or lockout is such as to prejudice a vital national interest.

In the event of a conflict arising in a national undertaking managing an essential public service, such as transportation, the stoppage of whose activities implies a risk of paralysing the economic life of the country or major urban centres, the public authorities intervene to end the strike. In public enterprises engaged in an economic activity in the same way as private undertakings, work stoppages are not supposed to affect the national interest. This is true, for example, for companies not having the status of public industrial or commercial establishment. Thus, a labour dispute should not in principle involve ipso facto government intervention.

In practice, collective disputes in general, whether they involve public or private enterprises, result, when they affect a fairly large number of workers, in intervention by the public authorities both locally (governor) and centrally (Minister of Social Affairs). Attempts have been made to resolve labour disputes by conciliation applying an emergency procedure very similar to arbitration. Judicial procedures are not always strictly applied.

The causes for collective disputes are the same for public and private enterprises. They mostly arise in connection with wage increases and related matters, career conditions and sometimes solidarity with union leaders or other workers.

In practice, disputes in public enterprises attract more attention than those in the private sector precisely because these undertakings employ the largest number of workers, provide public services and play a predominant role in the country's economic life. Strikes in these public enterprises may have repercussions on activities in a wide range of economic sectors and may sometimes constitute the main factor for a general strike. For instance, the strike by the UGTT on 26 January 1978, for the first time since Tunisia's independence, justified the use of personnel requisition decrees. This procedure which is provided under labour dispute legislation, had never been applied previously except in one specific case in 1977, when it was used against the Tunisian radio and television personnel.

The personnel of three national transport undertakings, railway, road and air, were requisitioned by Decree 78-48 of 25 January 1978. Another Decree, No. 78-47, of the same date, ordered the same measure in respect of the personnel of certain public enterprises which were either managing essential public services, such as the Tunisian Electricity and Gas Company (Société tunisienne de l'electricité et du gaz), the National Oil Distribution Company (Société nationale de distribution du pétrol), and the Tunisian Milk Industries Company (Société tunisienne des industries laitières), or occupying an important position in the economy, such as the Tunisian Iron and Steel Company (Société tunisienne de sidérurgie), cement companies, etc.

It can thus be seen that strikes in public enterprises have greater repercussions on national life than those affecting private undertakings and in all cases necessitate intervention by the public authorities, which seek to end them as rapidly as possible, generally by conciliation and only as an exceptional measure by requisition. So far, arbitration procedures have never been used, either at the request of the two parties or as a measure imposed by the public authority, because it was realised that these para-judicial procedures would not be very practical or effective.

It should be mentioned that more strikes occurred in 1977 than in the previous year. The following three tables relate to strikes in 1977 (no figures have been published concerning the general strike of 1978). There is no breakdown of figures for public and private enterprises, but it is clear that the former were more extensively affected due to the scale of their workforce and their importance for the economy.

Extent of strikes in 1976 and 1977

	1976	1977
No. of strikes	372	452
No. of undertakings	342	413
Total No. of workers employed	93 941	154 856
No. of workers involved	53 011	88 335
Proportion of coverage	56.43%	57.04%
Hours lost	1 043 012	1 207 482
Days lost	130 378	150 933
Hours lost per person	19.57	13.67
Individual days lost	2.45	1.71

Distribution of strikes by branch of activity, 1976-77

	1976	1977
Mines, energy	9	39
Agriculture and food industries	79	55
Textiles, clothing, leather	73	70
Wood, cork, furniture	18	12
Paper, miscellaneous industries	24	94
Chemical industries	29	33
Building materials, ceramics, glass	23	55
Mechanical and electrical industries	55	18
Buildings and public works	26	46
Transportation, storage	15	21
Miscellaneous	21	9
Total	372	452

Breakdown of strikes according to cause, 1976-77

Causes	1976	1977
Solidarity	123	154
Collective agreements and statutes	68	33
Wages and related matters	149	201
Conditions of work	72	74
Miscellaneous	27	47
Total	439	509

N.B.: 509 causes for 452 strikes, some strikes having several causes.

Mention should be made of the fact that in 1977, the Labour Inspectorate resolved 343 collective disputes involving 48,939 workers through its mediation services.

Chapter 4 - Personnel policy

Act 68-13 of 13 June 1968 establishing the general statute for public enterprises, the special statutes, the general collective agreement of 20 March 1973 and the special collective agreements for certain sectors contain provisions relating to career development, recruitment, promotion and discipline. Act 68-13 of 13 June 1968 provided that as a general rule recruitment shall be by competition and that in addition to external competitions open to all candidates there shall be internal competitions for existing personnel. A certain proportion of vacant posts, varying between 20 and 40 per cent, shall be reserved for internal competition, according to the job category. It is also permitted to make direct appointment by promotion for a maximum of 10 per cent of vacancies, in favour of persons in the category immediately below, included in a promotion table and possessing a certain seniority, of at least five years in the enterprise. These provisions governing recruitment in public enterprises are similar to the corresponding rules embodied in the civil service statute.

The special statutes and collective agreements provide that undertakings shall take measures for vocational training of workers, enabling them to improve their skills and advance in the heirarchy.

The basic collective agreement of 20 March 1973 and the sectoral collective agreements provide that recruitment for the various categories of personnel shall be carried out in accordance with the legislation in force. Collective agreements sometimes provide expressly for recruitment by competition, whereas they always provide for the possibility of filling posts by internal competition. Promotion is governed by a points system and submitted to a joint advisory committee. This procedure follows the pattern used in the general statute for public enterprises and that of the civil service (Acts 68-12 and 68-13 of 3 June 1968).

There are no provisions under Act 68-13 of 3 June 1968 regarding vocational training. On the other hand, the basic collective agreement stipulates that employers shall undertake to promote as far as possible appropriate training and advanced training. Where necessary, they must organise vocational training courses and apprenticeship training and do all that is possible to permit workers to receive normal and advanced training using all the measures considered most appropriate, in co-operation with the joint committee.

In practice, many sectoral collective agreements have in fact foreseen action to promote apprenticeship, vocational training, advanced training and retraining, special reference sometimes being made to the latter in the event of technological changes taking place within an undertaking. Furthermore, the public authorities have adopted measures to encourage heads of undertakings to take such actions. For example, it is stipulated in the Decree of 16 January 1957 that undertakings which take action for the technical or vocational training of their personnel may, on producing proof of the relevant expenditure, obtain a partial refund of the vocational training tax (2 per cent of wages paid) which they must pay annually to the State.

This provision applies to all enterprises public or private but in practice only the major undertakings (and these comprise practically all the public enterprises) possess the means to carry out vocational training which consists of organising training courses, training periods, and study fellowships in Tunisia or abroad. The banks and insurance companies, for example, organise continuous training courses for their staff. Some major enterprises, mostly public enterprises, have concluded agreements with the Tunisian Bureau for Expatriate Tunisian Workers, Employment and Vocational Training in order to organise vocational training centres of their own which would be administered in collaboration with the Bureau.

In order to encourage workers in their production effort and to improve output, the Government instituted a social progress prize and a model worker prize by two Decrees, 77-940 and 77-941 of 17 November 1977. These two prizes are open to all workers in all public or private undertakings with the exception of the public service proper. However, in practice, the vast majority of these prizes, which were awarded for the first time by an order of 27 June 1978, were awarded to public enterprises and their personnel.

Reference must also be made to the institution in some public enterprises of measures giving workers a share in profits. In the case of mining enterprises for example, it is provided by Act 66-45 of 4 July 1966 that 20 per cent of profits shall be distributed amongst the workers following proposals submitted by the promotion and classification committee.

In addition to the direct advantages which can be granted to workers, mention must also be made of other benefits given to them in the form of social welfare or social assistance. Public enterprises, like other undertakings governed by the basic or general collective agreement of 20 March 1973, have taken measures to increase the social advantages of their personnel. Wage earners enjoy the normal protection provided by the general law system as regards coverage for social risks, sickness, maternity, invalidity, old age, death, occupational accidents. Some public enterprises are in fact subject to the relevant legislation applicable to the private sector: Act 60-30 of 14 December 1960, as regards the general social security scheme (family benefits, social insurances, sickness, maternity, death); Decree 74-499 of 27 April 1974 as regards old age, invalidity and survivors' benefits: Act 57-73 of 11 December 1957 concerning occupational accidents and diseases. Other public enterprises are subject to the social legislation applicable to civil servants: Decrees of 12 April 1961 and Act 72-2 of 15 February 1972 relating to sickness; Act 57-18 of 5 February 1959 concerning retirement and Decree 74-572 of 22 May 1974 concerning death benefits.

Many undertakings, especially big ones, have endeavoured to improve the legal coverage for sickness by having group insurance which would enable their employees to obtain the reimbursement of medical costs, by organising mutual insurance groups providing the same services, or by establishing dispensaries to provide treatment for workers and members of their families.

In addition to such social security benefits, mention should be made of the provision of important social assistance policies. The institution of a social fund is at present becoming the rule in national undertakings. This is sometimes provided for in the statute and more usually created by decision of the board of management, approved by the responsible authorities. This fund is raised from large subsidies paid out of the undertaking's budget. It is designed to provide workers with social assistance in a number of ways such as: the organisation of a canteen or holiday camp groups; the granting of financial assistance in certain circumstances and particularly in the event of marriage or the beginning of a new school year; helping to have low interest loans especially for the purchase of accommodation or cars, and favourable interest rates for other loans, etc.

Chapter 5 - Participation by workers in decision making

Volume III, sections 157-169 of the Tunisian Labour Code embody the provisions of Act 60-31 of 14 December 1961 organising labour relations within undertakings, an Act which was based on the French law of 16 May 1946.

The Labour Code provides for the setting up of works committees for activities of any nature in which at least 50 wage earners are normally employed either directly or through a labour subcontractor. Works committees are thus compulsory in all public or private enterprises employing a minimum of 50 workers. A special board has been appointed to control the situation of undertakings in this connection and its decisions are submitted to the Ministry of Social Affairs for approval. If an undertaking is subject to the technical control of another department than that of the Ministry of Social Affairs, approval is the joint responsibility of this Ministry and the responsible Ministry. This is precisely the case for public enterprises, almost all of which are subject to the technical control of ministries other than that of social affairs.

Section 158 of the Labour Code provides that decrees issued on the proposal of the ministries concerned may establish special provisions relating to public enterprises of an industrial, commercial or agricultural nature, including services operated under State control, even monopolies, in respect of the composition, terms of reference and operation of the committees. In practice, such decrees have not been issued and the committees of public enterprises are organised on the same lines as those of private undertakings.

The Labour Code also stipulates that when the number of wage earners is less than 50 but more than 20, workers' delegates have to be nominated. This applies to all sectors. The members of works committees and workers' delegates are elected by the workers in application of the Decree of 13 January 1962, the provisions of which are now embodied in the Labour Code. The works committees have been given many administrative responsibilities. They have to co-operate with management in improving the general working and living conditions and education of the staff and of the relevant regulations. They have to supervise workers' health and safety. They are associated with the management of all social activities established within the undertaking for the benefit of the workers or their families, whatever the source of funds.

Regarding labour-management relations, the committees have to examine individual or collective claims and all difficulties arising between employer and worker. In this way they inevitably are familiar with different conditions which could lead to a collective labour dispute and to a strike or lockout.

At the economic level, the works committees have broad terms of reference which, if effectively applied, could transform the forms of economic organisation. Section 161 of the Labour Code, for example, stipulates that they must be consulted regarding the organisation of the undertaking so that they progressively become associated with its management and development. Taken to the limit, these powers could lead to the enhancement of democratic practices among workers. However, that stage has not yet been reached.

The works committees are also responsible for collaborating in the promotion and encouragement of increased output and greater production. They propose awards to workers who, by their initiative or suggestions have given useful assistance to the undertaking, and to those whose output has been exceptional. Inversely, they can propose sanctions against those who have not maintained normal output. It is to be noted that Decree 77-941 of 17 November 1977 has reinforced these provisions by creating a prize for outstanding workers.

In practice, many works committees (188, according to the inspection report for 1977) have effectively been established mainly in major public enterprises.

Workers' delegates who, in principle, must exist only in undertakings having between 20 and 50 workers, have been given responsibilities similar to those of the members of the works committee, although less binding as regards the organisation of the undertaking.

Apart from the works committees which may exist in all branches, the collective agreement of 20 March 1973 applicable only in the non-agricultural sector; foresees the setting up of a joint advisory commission in all establishments normally employing at least 20 workers, either directly or through branch companies. All sectoral collective agreements have applied this provision. The joint advisory commission has been given wide terms of reference, some of which duplicate those of the works committees (e.g. with respect to labour-management relations: application of administrative aspects of the collective agreement, ability to take care of all problems concerning the workers, participation in the adoption and application of provisions relating to social activities and, as regards economic matters, advising on the award of the productivity bonuses). The joint commission also has specific tasks of its own, such as: participating in personnel administration, establishment of rules for promotion and promotion lists, advising on changes in job allocation or the demotion of employees, promotion, transfer and discharge. It serves as a disciplinary board. It is also responsible for the study of problems concerning the entire workforce, particularly as regards apprenticeship, training and advanced training. It has to participate in the study and application of measures in connection with social welfare and retirement.

These provisions have been included regularly in the various sectoral collective agreements.

Many joint advisory commissions have been set up. In 1977 there were 658 for 1,410 undertakings employing over 20 workers, of which public enterprises constituted a large proportion.

Workers' representatives in undertakings generally have not yet been given the right to participate, as members of boards of management, in the administration of the undertaking, as they have in certain European countries.

In many public enterprises, the workers are not represented on the board of management, which consists only of representatives of the administration and of technicians, except in the case of certain large industrial or commercial public enterprises whose boards of management include workers representatives. The latter sometimes represent the personnel of the undertakings in question and are nominated on the basis of proposals from the union to which they belong, i.e. the UGTT. This applies to the board of management of the SNCFT, the STEG and the SNT, which are national undertakings managing public services, and even to certain public enterprises of an economic nature, such as SATPEC. It should be mentioned that these personnel representatives always constitute a minority of two out of eight or ten administrators.

In some bodies considered as public enterprises but which are really decentralised administrations, such as the National Social Security Board (CNSS) (Caisse nationale de la sécurité sociale) and the National Retirement Pensions and Social Security Board (CNRPS) (Caisse nationale des retraites et de prévoyance sociale), there are representatives not only of the undertakings' workers but also of the central workers' union, the UGTT. Nevertheless, co-ordination of views is achieved by internal consultations between the local and the central unions.

These two forms of participation certainly do not represent joint management, but a form of participation for workers. This is in fact useful for all the parties concerned, because it can help the workers to be better informed about problems faced by the undertaking in particular and the national economy in general. It is worth noting that representation of workers on boards of management is a normal governmental practice in Tunisia. The Central Union and Central Employers' Organisation constitute "national organisations" which guide the population, and their participation in management and decision making side by side with the Party's representatives is the general rule. This co-ordination has the effect of ensuring consultation with a view to achieving unanimity regarding decisions to be taken and of consolidating national unity in all sectors.

PART III - EVALUATION AND OUTLOOK

It can be expected that public enterprises will increase in number and spread throughout all branches. The philosophy of the leaders, national economic data and the attitude of the nation as a whole help to make public enterprises the driving force and main factor of the economic expansion which is a prerequisite for all social progress. Whenever a new need arises, the Government, aware of its responsibility in all fields, steps in and sets up new national undertakings, because private initiative is not sufficiently dynamic and does not always possess the necessary financial and legal means to satisfy all the needs of the society. For instance, the public authorities recently created by Act 78-44 of 1 August 1978 a Development Office for Central Tunisia and others may follow.

Public enterprises are not always profitable and some of these undertakings have had to cope with serious financial difficulties necessitating government assistance to cover the loss and redress the situation. In order to avoid large financial losses and to safeguard employment, the Government has taken a series of measures to improve the management and profitability of public enterprises. It has recommended that the managers of these undertakings be given greater stability so that they can see through long-term programmes.

The selection of these managers raises problems of ability and efficiency, as their posts have to be filled, taking into account technical know-how and not only on the basis of a militant service which may result in a second-rate personnel. In order to incite public enterprises to take an effective part in the implementation of the national economic plan, it has been recommended that the institution of a contract establishing a production programme between the management of the undertaking and the responsible ministry should be encouraged. Other measures also have been taken to ensure better operation of public enterprises, by associating boards of directors more closely with management and by regulating and adjusting the salaries of their managing directors. The accounts of these undertakings have to be published in the Official Gazette and this is one means of showing operational results clearly and of facilitating control by the public authorities and the National Assembly and judgement by informed citizens.

However, there appears to exist also a certain number of undertakings which operate at a profit. It should be noted that the incomes of public enterprises appeared in the State budget for 1978 in the section "State profits, interests and miscellaneous income" to the sum of 10.5 million dinars[1] which, for a total budgetary income of 541.2 million dinars, represents 1.94 per cent.

State control over a large part of the country's economic activities stems, as has been mentioned, from two trends:

(a) firstly, that of enabling the public authorities to manage directly those sectors considered as public services. This is really a question of avoiding the constraints of private capitalism in the management of public interest;

(b) secondly, that of developing the national economy whilst eliminating the possibility of private persons amassing unjustified income. The national undertakings may constitute a monopoly either de juris or de facto, or compete with private undertakings.

In the former case, the public enterprises tend to follow the lines of the public service. This explains why they have been granted statutes very similar to those of the public employees and officials, but are more generous as regards remuneration.

In the latter case, it was normal that despite the provisions of Act 68-13 of 3 June 1968, which covers all public enterprises, those with essentially economic objectives not considered as those of the public service, have tended to become undertakings in the private sector and have continued to be governed, as the latter, by the collective agreements and the Labour Code, particularly as regards labour-management relations.

State intervention in the setting up of undertakings is not expected to slow down or stop, because a growing population waking up to the needs of modern life would require the development of new activities in order to increase the volume of employment and raise the nation's living standards.

---

[1] One dinar equals approximately 0.53 US dollars (October 1981).

It would be in better conformity with democratic principles to associate workers' representatives to an increasing extent in the management of public enterprises. This would also be a better guarantee for peaceful and constructive labour-management relations and also a guarantee for efficiency in production. The workers would feel more concerned once they were sharing the responsibilities and problems of management. The effort demanded of them in order to increase production can be accepted more easily when they are not regarded as mere instruments, but rather as informed and conscious partners for progress.

www.ingramcontent.com/pod-product-compliance
Ingram Content Group UK Ltd.
Pitfield, Milton Keynes, MK11 3LW, UK
UKHW021322180426
11947UKWH00015B/1376